Biggin on The Bump

THE STORY OF THE MOST FAMOUS FIGHTER STATION IN THE WORLD

by Bob Ogley

It was the pilots of the Second World War who called it "The Bump". Returning from a sortie above the orchards, or a patrol over the Channel, they would fly across the Weald of Kent towards the chalk hills of the North Downs and, at the highest point, look for a terribly scarred concrete runway. This was Biggin Hill, "home" until the next scramble. Just a tiny patchwork square of England, but a beautiful sight. Biggin Hill is a name comparable to Alamein in epoch-making glory for it was one of the ramparts from which The Few launched their attack against the Luftwaffe. It guarded the southern approaches to London and its aces, flying Hurricanes and Spitfires, shot down more than 1,600 enemy aircraft. This book provides a unique photographic record of the men, women, machines and indomitable spirit which made Biggin Hill the most famous fighter station in the world.

> Author's royalties will be donated to the RAF Benevolent Fund on behalf of RAF Biggin Hill.

Froglets Publications 1990

Published in Great Britain by Froglets Publications Limited,
Brasted Chart, Westerham, Kent TN16 1LY
Telephone: (0959) 62972. Fax: (0959) 65365

First impression May 1990

Reprinted June 1990

© Bob Ogley 1990

ISBN 1-872337-05-8 (Paperback) 1-872337-10-4 (Hardback)

Cover illustrations:
Front cover: Once more . . . . Adlertag
August 15, 1940, by Frank Wootton
A print of this painting may be obtained on application to Commemorative Promotions Ltd., (Fine Art Print) 43 Grove Park Rd., London W4 3UR.

Back cover:
The legends of Biggin Hill by Bob Murray.
Prints available on request to the Publishers.
Top Row: F2B Fighter, Gloster Grebes, Bristol Bulldog. Middle Row: SE5A, Spitfire, Gloster Gladiator. Bottom Row: Avro Tutor Hawker Hart, Gloster Gauntlet.

This book was fully produced by
Pen & Ink Publicity Services,
9 Cannon Lane, Tonbridge, Kent TN9 1PP.
Casebound by BPCC Hazell Books.

A special thank you to Fern who helped with the research, took many colour photographs and was greatly involved in the production at all stages.

Photographs credited to RAF Biggin Hill have been collected over the years from a variety of sources.

Environmentally friendly paper 40% straw, without chlorine.

Acknowledgements

This year, 1990, marks the 50th anniversary of the Battle of Britain and this book has been produced to celebrate that historic milestone and, on behalf of RAF Biggin Hill, raise much-needed funds for the RAF Benevolent Fund. The author wishes to thank the officers at Biggin Hill whose inspiration it was that a history be published, reproducing the unique photographs that existed in their archives.

It became apparent that most of these remarkable pictures were taken during the war and considerably more were required for a comprehensive photographic history. The Imperial War Museum have supplied many of the photographs as have most of those listed below.

I would particularly like to thank Avril Oswald for reading the copy and undertaking additional research, Ken Owen of the Kent Aviation Historical Society for his vigilance in checking facts, Frank Wootton and Bob Murray for their wonderful paintings, John Freeman and Kath Preston for access to their albums, and, in particular, Jill Goldsworthy, Alison Stammers, Flight Lieutenant Verena McLean and SAC Matt Smith. David Porter of Shoreham, Kent has given much valuable advice in the preparation of this book and I thank him most sincerely.

I am also most grateful to the following: John Nelson, the Nevard family, David Linton, Ted Surgison, Robin Brooks, Doug Geer, John Cullimore, Mark Lance, Clive Brown, Gordon Anckorn, Squadron Leader Jock Maitland, Fiona Wright of Bromley Library, Dennis Knight, Jack Marriott and Geoffrey Nutkins.

I would particularly like to thank the fighter pilots for allowing me to impose on their time in a year of interviews, engagements, broadcasts and reunions, particularly Alan Deere, R. Deacon Elliott, Peter Brothers, Ken Campbell, Donald Stones, Desmond Sheen, Harbourne Stephens, Douglas Grice, Ian Cosby, Johnny Johnson, Jack Rose, Ronald Hamlyn, Tom Gleave and Pat Hancock of the Battle of Britain Fighters' Association. To that list of heroes I add the heroines, Dame Felicity Peake (previously Hanbury), Elspeth Green (nee Henderson) and Joan Elizabeth Mortimer.

Finally a big thank you to Brian Kingcome who has supplied a superb account of his days at his favourite fighter station.

The strongest link

The Royal Air Force Biggin Hill badge on page one shows a sword, ringed by a circlet of chain. The sword, unsheathed with point upward, is a fighting sword, symbolic of the famous part played by the Station in the Battle of Britain. The blood-red colour is also symbolic of fighting and of the warriors, in this case winged, who took part in the Battle. A connotation with the sword of St Paul, which is of similar design and colour and which is displayed in the Arms of the City of London, also is evident, Biggin Hill having played a key part in the defence of the capital against the Luftwaffe. It is of interest, too, to note that St George of England's sword was a fighting one; and that the evocative St George's Chapel at Biggin Hill also commemorates the Station's part in the Battle of Britain. The circlet of chain, in gold to indicate quality, symbolises the ring of Royal Air Force Stations which then defended the capital city. The motto, *The Strongest Link*, alludes to the fact that Biggin Hill claimed over one thousand enemy aircraft destroyed during World War II.

Chester Herald, College of Arms

Biggin on The Bump

MUCH has already been written about RAF Biggin Hill and little wonder. It has a history so fascinating, so colourful, so dramatic and so romantic that it is sometimes difficult to believe that it is a true story.

It was from Biggin Hill that Bristol Fighters operated at night against Gotha bombers in the last year of the 1914-18 war. It was from Biggin Hill that wireless pioneers made the first communication between the ground and aircraft in flight. It was at Biggin Hill that the army's air defence unit was established, where the early pre-radar dishes were constructed, where night flying was perfected and where three operational squadrons were billetted to help protect London and the south-east from the growing Nazi menace.

In this book an attempt has been made to tell all of these stories, and many more, by publishing photographs, obtained from the archives at RAF Biggin Hill and other aviation sources. There are more than 200. Many are famous pictures which have appeared in other publications over the years; the majority, however, have never been published.

By telling the story of Biggin Hill in this form it has not been possible to give a thoroughly detailed history. That has been achieved by other authors, notably Graham Wallace and Nicholas Wright and I commend "RAF Biggin Hill" and "The Bump" to all students of aviation literature.

This photographic history of "Biggin on The Bump" has been published to celebrate the 50th anniversary of the most famous period in the station's history — The Battle of Britain. It is hoped that these pictures will revive the memories, for those who were alive, of the vital contribution Biggin Hill made to the defence of our country during that long hot summer of 1940 — and beyond.

It is important to stress that 52 different squadrons flew under the colours of the Biggin Hill Wing during the war; that hundreds of airmen were billetted on "The Bump", some for just days, others for many years. Every one of those courageous young men is worth a book but, sadly, it has not been possible to do justice to them all. Nor has it been possible to give adequate space and attention to those who worked behind the scenes; the fitters, mechanics, controllers, drivers, administrators, caterers, civilian personnel and those lovely, cheerful WAAFs who played their part in winning the war.

Fifty years ago Britain was in a desperate crisis. She survived because of the armed forces, particularly the Royal Air Force, particularly those who flew from "Biggin on The Bump".

Contents

Various maps, charts and statistics which may be helpful in following the history of Biggin Hill are contained on . .

BIGGIN HILL 1917

Cudham School

Fox & Hounds Inn

Buckhurst Lodge

HAWLEY'S CORNER

South Street Farm

Great South Street Farm

SOUTH STREET

Brickyard Farm

Jail Lane

Lodge

PIMLICO

Costain's Farm

Aperfield Court

Lodge

Old House

Cudham Lodge

AREA OF CAMPS

Koonowla

Black Horse Inn

BIGGIN HILL

Smithy

Polesteeple Hill

King's Arms Inn

LEAVES GREEN

Lodge

Ivy Cottages

N

Saltbox

Line of Roman Road

Norheads Farm

Jewels Wood

Skid Hill Farm

Biggin Hill in 1917 showing the area taken over by the Wireless Testing Park and Aperfield Court, a spacious mansion where a transmitter was installed for the ground-to-air control of fighters defending London in the 1914-18 war. (Photograph: John Nelson)

4

A Hawker Demon of 23 Squadron flies over the Salt Box at Biggin Hill in 1933, the year that Hitler came to power. At the time Winston Churchill was worried about weakness in the air. "Only a strong British Air Force," he said, "can protect Britain from invasion and defeat." This picture shows the road between Bromley and Westerham at the spot where a pioneer parachutist, Corporal East was killed (see page 22) and is supplied by Mrs Doll Scott.

Winston Churchill at Biggin Hill in RAF uniform

WING Commander Charles Brian Kingcome DSO DFC was posted to Biggin Hill as a Flight Commander with 92 Squadron on September 8, 1940 in the middle of the Battle of Britain and just one week after the station had been virtually obliterated by the Luftwaffe. In combat "Kingpin", as he was called, "drove the train" and inspired his Squadron to become one of the most renowned in Fighter Command. With 130 destroyed, 60 probables and 70 damaged they were easily the top scoring Squadron to be stationed at Biggin Hill. Here, Brian Kingcome tells what it was like to live and fly in those grim days of 1940 and how and why he developed a very special affection for "Biggin on The Bump".

'The gratitude of every home in our island, in our Empire, and indeed throughout the world, except in the abodes of the guilty, goes out to the British airmen who, undaunted by odds, unwearied in their constant challenge and mortal danger, turned the tide of the world war by their prowess and by their devotion. Never in the field of human conflict was so much owed by so many to so few.'

The way it was

"What did you do in the war, Daddy?"
"Got drunk in the White Hart at Brasted, my son."

NOT all the time, perhaps, but it was certainly not unknown. And in the early 1940's before plastic rusticity became the vogue, the White Hart at Brasted, the pub we used as our local during my days at Biggin Hill, was as congenial a place as any to do it in.

No doubt about it, of all the members of the fighting forces during the last war, the fighter pilot, and especially the Spitfire pilot, had the most enviable of jobs. Not for him the endless tension and terror endured by the convoy patrols in the Atlantic and the North Sea, of the bomber pilot deep into enemy territory and at the mercy of any half-trained Bavarian peasant at the end of an anti-aircraft gun, of the sub-mariner listening for the depth charges crouched in his claustrophobic hole, and of the countless other fighting men who faced acute danger and discomfort over long periods of time.

'Ahead of us was life, at least until the next telephone call. Electrifying adrenalin filled life. One long sustained high.'

The Spitfire pilot in 1940, charged with the defence of his homeland, faced a longish day, of course — from half an hour before dawn to half an hour after dusk — but he flew from a warm and comfortable base with the most versatile of all fighter aircraft, and being a single seater he was more or less master of his own fate. I suppose at the height of the Battle of Britain we averaged three, sometimes four, sorties a day, but a sortie seldom lasted more than an hour, and we had the immense moral advantage of fighting over our own territory. Surprising how fierce one's protective instincts become at the sight of an enemy violating one's homeland, and how comforting the knowledge that if one is shot down one at least has a chance of living to fight another day.

Contrast this with the wretched German pilot, flying at the extreme end of his range, over hostile territory, and for the first time in his hitherto all-conquering operational life up against a fighter aircraft comparable if not superior to his own. No wonder the poor chaps couldn't wait for winter and a break in the weather.

And of all the places from which to operate, as I did from August 1940 to June 1942, Biggin Hill was way out front. It was superbly placed, both operationally and socially. Operationally we were just far enough inland from the main German approach lanes to give us time to climb flat out due north to the enemy's altitude before turning south to hit him head on, by far the most effective and damaging form of attack, usually somewhere over mid-Kent.

Socially it exhausts me just thinking about it. When we were stood down half an hour after dusk there was the choice of either scooting up to London, where ten shillings (the bulk of our day's pay of 14 shillings) would cover an evening at Shepherds and the Bag of Nails (the Four Hundred if we could raise a quid), or the White Hart at Brasted, where five shillings kept us in beer until the local bobby moved us on at closing time. Then with a few girl friends on to our billets, a comfortable local country house where we were dispersed at night against the possibility of an air attack on the airfield (all that money that had gone into our training couldn't be put at risk) where one of our pilots, a pianist who could hold his own against any night club musician and frequently did, would play into the small hours, and we would finally snatch an hour or two's sleep in armchairs, fully dressed to save time and effort getting up for dawn readiness.

Then the dispersal hut with the unforgettable sound of Merlin engines warming up in the grey half-light, the squadron doctor dispensing his miracle hangover cure (would that I had kept the recipe) from a tin bucket, occasionally a pilot, suffering more than usual, climbing into his cockpit for a quick rejuvenating whiff of neat oxygen. And then the inevitable, stomach churning ring of the telephone and the voice from ops: "92 Squadron, scramble. One hundred plus bandits approaching Dungeness at angels fifteen".

The surge of adrenalin, the half dozen or so pilots that were all that we could normally muster sprinting to their aircraft, the tiredness and the hangovers disappearing as though they had never been and the flat out climb to twenty thousand feet. The mud on our flying boots would freeze hard to our rudder bars in our unheated and unpressurised cockpits, but as we saw the sun lift over the horizon at twenty thousand feet, it was a hard turn south east to meet the enemy, the swarm of bees against the lightening sky swiftly transforming into a phalanx of bombers as the gap between us magically closes, tier upon tier with their escorting fighters weaving above, forcing one's voice on the R/T to remain calm and relaxed.

"Gannet Squadron, spread out and pick your targets". The bomber pilots would already be getting jittery at this attack on their most exposed and vulnerable quarter with nothing between them and our guns except a thin sheet of perspex, the tracer curling out at us, the sound of our own guns like tearing calico, bombers dropping smoking out of formation, three or four seconds of ammunition of our precious fifteen already gone, then into the clear air behind suddenly filled with more aircraft as the enemy fighters hit us from above, the whirling dog-fight with friend and foe almost indistinguishable, the last of one's ammunition gone and the sky suddenly empty.

For those of us safely back on the still darkened earth the sun would rise again. The day was only just beginning and already behind us a lifetime of action packed into an hour, death, the memory of two sunrises in one morning and thoughts quickly suppressed of friends not yet accounted for. And ahead of us life, at least until the next telephone call. Electrifying, adrenalin filled life. One long, sustained high.

I remember Biggin Hill with enormous affection. The strange double life, each one curiously detached from the other. One moment high above the earth watching a sunrise not yet visible below, killing and avoiding being killed; and the next chatting with the locals over a pint of beer in a cosy country pub as casually as though we had just stepped off the 6 o'clock from Waterloo after a day in the City. Occasionally a local commenting critically on the aerial activity he had witnessed that day as though he were discussing his local football team. And the next morning back to the unreal world and the twisting smoke trails at angels two-five. This could only happen to a fighter pilot.

Of course there were intensely sad moments as well as intensely exciting ones. I lost many old friends as well as making many new ones, and the worst part was watching them die, spiralling down with a smudge of smoke, or breaking up, watching for the parachute to blossom, the relief when it did, the sick feeling when it didn't.

I walk with ghosts when I re-visit my old station, but they are friendly ones. I mourn them, but they had counted the cost and they died with regret but without surprise. They were typical of their generation, and their generation was typical of all others. The young of all generations are the same. They may dress differently and have different rites and rituals, but give them a crisis and they are all the same.

I salute them.

Brian Kingcome

1. BIRTH OF THE BUMP

1916-17

THE story of Biggin Hill began in the summer of 1916 when two subalterns from the Wireless Testing Park at Joyce Green, Dartford were instructed to look for an alternative site. Their travels took them to Biggin Hill, or Aperfield as it was then known, a hamlet high on the North Downs between Westerham and Bromley. There, they found a flat field of 75 acres. It was the perfect site.

Two years after the outbreak of war, the Royal Flying Corps (RFC) had foreseen the possibility of wireless communication in aviation. They desperately needed a site for an aerodrome where vital equipment could be tested. It needed to be fog free, high enough for a range of signals to be tested without interruption and large enough for intensive flying.

The subalterns, Lieutenants Hanzard and Furnival found that the site at Biggin Hill was almost on the Prime Meridian yet only 17 miles south of London Bridge. More important it was one of the highest points in Kent, 600 feet above sea level on the chalk escarpment of the North Downs. What better place to develop a system of communication with pilots in the air? The idea received the backing of the War Office and on December 2, 1916, official sanction was given for the re-siting of the Wireless Testing Park at Biggin Hill.

The land there formed part of Cudham Lodge, a Georgian mansion owned by Earl Stanhope of Chevening and tenanted by John Westacott. Stanhope, himself an army officer, had already agreed that part of his land could be used as a night emergency landing ground. He happily relinquished several more acres.

Close to the field on the Westerham to Bromley road was a large brick house known as Koonowla. It had been bequeathed to the Victorian Hospital for Sick Children at Chelsea and the trustees were anxious to keep the house and its accompanying endowment. The RFC considered it would make an ideal Mess so the War Office invoked the Defence of the Realm Act and Koonowla became part of the Biggin Hill complex.

By February 13, 1917, the transfer of officers and men from Joyce Green was completed. Wooden huts and tents were erected, a canvas hangar was put up and the officers quartered in Koonowla. The first airmen had already arrived. Lieutenant Dickie and Air Mechanic Chadwick flew in with an RE7 on a bitterly cold January day and landed in thick snow.

As the two men climbed out of the aeroplane they were greeted by a flurry of snowballs. History had been made. They were the first men to land at "Biggin on the Bump".

Koonowla had been a hospital for sick children. In 1916 it became the Officers' Mess at Biggin Hill. (Photograph: John Nelson)

Officers of The Royal Flying Corps whose pioneering work at Biggin Hill paved the way for wireless communication between the ground and aircraft in flight. Before the end of the 1914-18 war, movement of Home Defence Squadrons in the air was being controlled through the transmitter at Biggin Hill. (Photograph: Imperial War Museum)

School of Telephony

1917

THE Commander of the Royal Flying Corps, Major General "Boom" Trenchard realised that speed was essential in developing wireless telephony for use in aviation and he gave every encouragement to the officers at Biggin Hill, who tested, rejected and occasionally approved equipment produced at Woolwich. The camp buzzed with activity; research led to practical experiments but the scientists found great difficulty in developing a system which met Trenchard's stringent requirements.

Many hours' work was put in by these wireless pioneers. At times there was high excitement and then sheer frustration as something went wrong. There were experiments with valves, microphones, receivers, aerials and Biggin Hill was soon festooned with wires. Eventually a system was installed in a BE2e and the voice of the operator was heard in a second aeroplane. The sound was distorted but it was a measure of success.

There were more experiments and more adjustments. Earphones were introduced and new flying helmets designed with built-in pockets for the microphone and earphone. In July, 1917, Lieutenant Furnival in a Sopwith 1½ Strutter clearly heard the words spoken by Lieutenant Andrews in a similar aircraft. Furnival's pilot, Captain Richard Peck dipped his wing in acknowledgement and increased the distance between the two aircraft. Andrews' voice continued to be heard. After many failures air-to-air wireless telephony was, at last, a reality.

Trenchard, delighted, congratulated Biggin Hill on the success of the experimental work and the design of the apparatus. Twenty sets were immediately produced, tested at Biggin Hill and fitted to the Bristol Fighters flown by No 11 Squadron in France. Trenchard then instructed Lieutenant Furnival to organise a school of wireless telephony.

Britain was first to develop this system of air-to-air wireless contact. Biggin Hill had beaten the Germans.

An RE7 biplane, 140hp, was the first aircraft to land at Biggin Hill in January 1917.

"D" Flight of 39 Squadron flew in from Hornchurch in December 1917. Equipped with BE2e's they were commanded by Captain A.B. Fanstone. (Photographs: Imperial War Museum)

Defending London

1917-18

THE threat to Britain from an enemy in the skies had existed from the time that Louis Bleriot flew the Channel in 1909 and England, it was feared, was no longer an island. This became alarmingly clear when the German Navy and Army produced an amazing airship invented by Count Ferdinand von Zeppelin.

In 1912 Britain created the Royal Flying Corps with naval and military wings but by the time war broke out in 1914 the army was charged with the air defence of the United Kingdom and devoted most of its efforts to the operational squadrons in France.

As war progressed Zeppelin airships were introduced as bombing platforms, the first attack coming on January 19, 1915 when bombs were dropped on Kings Lynn and several Norfolk villages. In May that year London suffered its first Zeppelin attacks. Exactly two years later a new sturdy twin-engine bomber, the Gotha, scattered bombs over Kent. One stick fell in Folkestone killing 56 women and children.

On June 13, 1917, 14 Gothas penetrated the heart of London, unloaded their bombs on Liverpool Street station and headed home with no challenge from the Royal Flying Corps.

As the intensity of the German raids increased and the casualties mounted, six squadrons of British fighters were diverted from France to defend London. Zeppelin raids virtually ceased and the Gothas switched from daylight to night attacks. Forced to take the shortest route to London because of their limited range the Gothas flew over the Wireless Testing Park at Biggin Hill.

The nightly raids and the inadequacy of the defence caused a public outcry. Searchlights were introduced, work was begun on sound locators and barrage fire became more accurate. As the winter of 1917-18 approached and the prospects of raids increased, two additional home defence squadrons were sanctioned. One of them, 141 Squadron, was to be stationed at Biggin Hill.

Time was needed to recruit, equip and organise a new fighter squadron and South London could not be left undefended. So "D" Flight of 39 Squadron was despatched from Hornchurch with BE2e's and BE12's to hold the fort at Biggin Hill. This squadron set up a tented camp on the north-west side of the airfield, made several uneventful sorties against Gothas and on February 8, 1918, joined forces with 141 Squadron — the first operational squadron at Biggin Hill.

Two months later, on April 1, the Royal Flying Corps and the Royal Naval Air Service were merged into a new Royal Air Force. The raids on London, which killed hundreds and dealt a blow to national pride, were behind the birth of the RAF.

Soldiers guard the wreckage of the Gotha bomber which crashed at Frinsted, a village to the south of Sittingbourne. The villagers, like others in south-east England, had often seen the German raiders high in the skies, seemingly oblivious to any defence measures. On May 20, 1918 they were privileged to have proof of the raiders' vulnerability. (Photograph: William Smith)

The first 'kill'

May 1918

SOMETIME after 10.30 on the night of May 19, 1918, holidaymakers on the east Kent coast, enjoying a moonlight bathe, saw a flare float down over the sea. It was the signal for an air raid and within 30 minutes an attacking force of 38 Gothas, three Riesen (Giants) and two smaller planes were crossing the Channel and heading for the Thames estuary.

Warning maroons were fired in London and searchlights switched on. High angle anti-aircraft guns were trained on the starlit sky as the raiders droned towards the capital with their deadly cargo.

In the Operations Room at Biggin Hill, news of the raid — the biggest of the 1914-18 war — was received from Central Control. 141 Squadron took off in Bristol Fighters (Brisfits) to intercept the bombers. By now almost half of the attacking force had got through to London, released their bombs and were returning to base in Belgium.

Lieutenants E.E. Turner (pilot) and H.B. Barwise (observer) were flying at 12,000 feet some two miles east of Biggin Hill when they spotted the unmistakeable shape of a Gotha above them. It was flying at 87 mph and had, so far, met no challenge from the British fighters ordered into the air.

Turner, keeping his eyes fixed on the Hun, climbed high to gain altitude and then screamed down, pouring incendiary tracer bullets into the Gotha. Barwise had the raider in the sights of his Lewis gun and splayed it furiously from nose to tail. Nothing happened. No flames appeared so Turner manoeuvred his Brisfit for a second attack. For a few seconds the pilot lost his prey and then saw it below losing height rapidly.

Major Sowrey, Commanding Officer of 143 Squadron in a Camel saw the wounded Gotha and attacked it again. Out of control it crash-landed at Frinsted in Kent. The pilot and navigator were killed but the rear gunner escaped with a broken arm.

Who had registered the first kill, the Brisfit or the Camel? For more than 24 hours victory celebrations were postponed at Biggin Hill until Wing Headquarters had investigated the incident. They interviewed the injured gunner in hospital and he confirmed that the fatal damage had been caused by the Brisfit. Turner and Barwise were the heroes of the hour.

This was Biggin Hill's first "kill" as a fighter station. The men of 141 Squadron celebrated in the Mess where they heard that more German night raiders had perished — three to the guns, two more to fighters, another down from engine failure and three more crash-landed in Belgium.

It was to be the last air attack of the 1914-18 war. The Germans decided enough was enough. The defences had mastered the bomber and Biggin Hill had played a vital role in world peace.

Cock Squadron

1918

GERMANY'S decision to abandon the bombing of England and concentrate all resources on the desperate struggle in France and Belgium meant a quiet life for the squadrons of the London Air Defence Force.

The average age of the young men of 141 Squadron was only 21 and many had just returned from the Western Front where the life expectancy of a pilot was barely 11 days. Now back in England they hated their enforced period of inactivity and boredom began to set in.

Those who survived the deadly aerial combats in France to form the new 141 Squadron included Australians, Canadians, New Zealanders, Rhodesians and a Sikh, Lieutenant Hardit Singh Malik who always wore his turban under his flying hat.

Although they were relieved from the strains of flying they found it necessary to make up their own wild fun and games, their "opponents" being the wireless officers in the other camp. On one occasion they turned their attention to a large wooden teapot hanging outside the village teashop. 141 despatched a midnight raiding party to acquire the trophy and incurred the wrath of the Wireless Experimental Establishment who organised a counter-raid to snatch it back. Back and forth it went until the owner of the teashop called in to collect his property.

The summer months passed slowly. The men who had come to expect a short but dangerously exciting life found themselves playing rugby, cross country running and organising wild drinking contests in the Mess. On one dramatic occasion a game of airborne rummy was arranged in a captured AEG German bomber. This twin-engine machine could carry up to six and was in great demand for joy riding. The game ended when the propeller flew off and the machine went into a tight spin. Major Baker who was at the controls managed to land the AEG and then condemned it to the scrap heap.

In France the character of the war was changing. Tanks were now

141 Squadron in March 1918

spearheading the initial attacks while allied planes struck at German infantry columns. The newly-formed RAF put up a magnificent show in these last crucial stages of the Great War but the squadrons at home fretted with frustration.

To keep up morale, the General commanding the VIth London Defence Brigade, Brigadier General T.C.R. Higgins organised a Squadron-at-Arms competition. All units in the Command were to participate in formation flying, aerobatics, wireless telephony, gunnery and a *Concours d'Elegance* of machines, airfields and buildings. The winning squadron would receive a silver cup, the title of Cock Squadron and the rights to display the fighting cock emblem on their aircraft.

At first 141 Squadron was reluctant to enter but quickly picked up the competitive spirit, succeeded in the eliminating rounds and came out as Cock Squadron in the final at Suttons Farm in Essex, an aerodrome occupied by 78 Squadron. After the event they took off in triumph for Biggin Hill but tragically one Bristol Fighter crashed, killing both pilot and observer.

The Cock Squadron proudly display the live bird which was presented to them by Mr and Mrs Nevard of The Salt Box, Biggin Hill.
(Photograph: Imperial War Museum)

13

Not the first aircraft to land at Biggin Hill, but the first to be stationed there, a Sopwith 1½ Strutter, with part of the casing removed. The picture shows Flight Sergeant Draper the pilot, with Bobby Wright in the passenger seat, Murray has his hands on the blade of the propeller and Flight Mechanic Al Chadwick, extreme right, was one of the first two people to land at "The Bump". All the young men were billetted on Mrs Doll Scott at the Salt Box, who kindly provided the picture and the identification, at the age of 94.

Old Salt Box, Cudham Kent (Front View).

The Salt Box is a name that will always be synonymous with Biggin Hill, for this unique building with its tall roof was a landmark for pilots from 1916 until it was demolished just after the Battle of Britain. The building was originally two farm cottages and became a popular tea room before being taken over by the RAF in 1936. Lieutenant Hardit Singh Malik, the Sikh from Rawalpindi was billetted at the Salt Box with his batman in 1918. He earned the nickname of the 'flying hobgoblin'. (Photograph: John Nelson)

End of hostilities

November 1918

AT dawn on the morning of November 11, 1918, a party of German politicians and army generals entered a guarded railway carriage in the forest of Compiegne. A few hours later at 11 am the Armistice was signed. After four and a half years of bloody fighting the guns fell silent on the battlefields of Europe.

Ever since the Allies had broken through the German lines and forced the enemy to retreat, England had been waiting anxiously for news of the surrender. It came in the most unexpected way. A wireless operator at Aperfield Court, Biggin Hill, seeking news from France, tuned into the Eiffel Tower station and picked up a message from Marshal Foch to all C in C's. The message was quite straightforward. "Hostilities will cease on the whole Front as from November 11 at 11 o'clock (French time)."

The operator, one of the first to learn of the good tidings, told Major Baker who alerted the local padres. Within minutes the bells of Westerham and Cudham were pealing — the first in all Britain to proclaim the end of hostilities. No-one questioned why the bells pealed so merrily. It was instantly known that peace had come at last. The scenes of public revelry and rejoicing which began in Westerham, Cudham and Biggin Hill swept through the country within minutes.

John Westacott at Cudham Lodge heard the bells, sounded the "View Halloo", galloped across to the North Camp and rode his hunter round and round the billiard table. Aircraft came out of the hangars and pilots gave joy rides over Bromley and Sevenoaks to all the Biggin Hill girls. Major Baker announced a day's leave.

A group of pilots and wireless operators from Biggin Hill decided to 'invade' London. They burst into the Savoy, demanding champagne and whooping like Indians. Officers from 141 Squadron then dragged the guns in Hyde Park down The Mall and left them lying under Admiralty Arch. In Trafalgar Square the Cock Squadron started a bonfire which left its scars on the base of Nelson's Column. Later that night the two units from Biggin Hill, the fighter pilots and the wireless officers had a rendezvous at the Savoy. They took over the band and formed a wild crocodile dancing through and over the tables reserved for generals. An elderly guest, watching the fun, enjoyed himself so much that he footed the bill for all the broken crockery and glass.

Next day London was declared out of bounds to the men of 141 Squadron. They obeyed the order and instead created mayhem in Croydon.

British military aircraft became known as Fokker fodder during the 1914-18 war, especially during the battle of The Somme where the Red Baron, von Richthofen and his colleagues caused such havoc. Little wonder there was so much interest among the young airmen at Biggin Hill in this captured Fokker DV11 (160 hp). (Photograph: Imperial War Museum)

2. BETWEEN THE WARS

SOON after the fusion of the Royal Flying Corps and the Royal Naval Air Service into the RAF, the decision was made to concentrate all wireless research at Biggin Hill. The RNAS establishment at Cranwell closed, the work of the Royal Engineers at Woolwich was transferred and Lieutenant Colonel L.F. Blandy DSO assumed command of the WEE — now greatly expanded.

Work began on permanent buildings for the South Camp in March 1918 and plans were drawn up for an Officers' Mess, barrack blocks, laboratories and concrete hangar, a project that was to cost £220,000, take two years to complete and cause great bitterness among those forced to live in appalling conditions.

There was a scandal over the high wages paid to labourers and the fact that local farmers were left with a shortage of workers. So serious did it become that Godstone Rural Council protested to the Air Ministry about the London trade union rate of over £4 a week which was being paid to airfield labourers.

As the WEE expanded new aeroplanes were flown — twin engine bombers Handley Page 0/400 and DH 10s — and more fields were requisitioned for lengthening the runways.

By now Biggin Hill employed almost 600 including 68 officers, 297 men and 228 members of the Women's Royal Air Force. One of the greatest personalities was a retired ancient mariner, Captain Uriah Cook. Attached to the Mess he was affectionately known as 'Barnacle Bill', no task was too great for him and he was loved by all.

Meanwhile work on the rebuilding of the site continued but living conditions for the young wireless research staff were appalling. More than 500 were forced to live in tents or in the few leaking huts that remained. The winter of 1918-19 was long and hard. There was no heating, no hot water, mud everywhere and the food was totally unsatisfactory.

In January 1919 the men met to discuss their plight and recommended an all-out strike. Some wanted a gentlemanly approach but others sang the Red Flag at the top of their voices and suggested violence. Mutiny was in the air. They would march down Piccadilly and present their case to the Air Ministry.

Eventually the RAF decided to investigate the labour unrest and instructed Brigadier General A.C.H. McLean to talk to the men. He listened to what they had to say, then toured the Camp. He was appalled. He spoke to the builders, threatening to cancel their contract unless they promised to put everything right. He then called together all the officers and men of the WEE and announced they could go on leave while their camp was improved.

When they returned, refreshed and grateful, South Camp looked a great deal more habitable. The mutiny was over.

Air defence at Biggin Hill at the end of the 1914-18 war. Captain Uriah Cooke, better known as Barnacle Bill is in front in civilian clothing.

The first public demonstration of air-to-ground wireless telephony by 141 Squadron. This took place at Suttons Farm, an airfield in Essex where the Cock Squadron won the Concours d'Elegance. (Photograph: RAF Biggin Hill)

Hello Newport *1919*

AN event which took place in the House of Lords in August 1919 demonstrated the value of Biggin Hill as a research station and left an assembly of peers, MP's, Treasury officials and RAF officers enthusing over the capabilities of the marvellous new technology known as The Wireless.

The demonstration was set up to show just what could be carried through the atmosphere by wireless waves. It began with an operator at Aperfield Court, Biggin Hill reciting some verses followed by the rousing chords of the 1812 Overture. For many of the distinguished guests this was the first broadcast they had ever heard and they looked at the great horn in front of them in growing disbelief. Was it a hoax? The Under Secretary of State for Air, Major General Seely, assured them it wasn't. "You are about to hear an historic broadcast which has never before been given."

The audience which included Lord Trenchard stared hard at the loudspeaker carrying the voice of Lieutenant S.G. Newport, a wireless officer. "I am in an aircraft", he told them.

Seely replied: "Hello Newport. We are in the Houses of Parliament. Can you hear us?"

"Hello Houses of Parliament. I can hear you well. My pilot can hear you too. We are flying at 8,000 feet, 20 miles away."

The Speaker of the House then held a brief conversation with Newport before handling the microphone back to Seely who boldly invited all pilots who had taken off from Biggin Hill and were flying within 20 miles of London to dine with him at the House of Commons. The message was picked up and, one by one, the pilots accepted the invitation to dinner.

As a pioneer broadcast it was brilliantly executed and the staff at the Wireless Experimental Station at Biggin Hill quietly congratulated themselves on the part they had played in broadcasting history.

The Government was also impressed and sanctioned the Treasury to set up an Instrument Design Establishment at Biggin Hill.

The IDE remained at Biggin Hill for four successful years, carrying out a series of experiments in long distance flying and landing aircraft in thick mist and fog. Significant research projects included the construction of a giant concrete disc emitting a high-pitched sound to guide in the pilot. The deafening noise terrified cattle and shattered windows for miles around.

Eventually the IDE was amalgamated with the Royal Aircraft Establishment and moved to Farnborough. Lord Trenchard was now able to pursue one of his greatest wishes — that Biggin Hill should become solely a fighter station and help to shape the future air defence of Great Britain.

A Handley Page 0/400 was the aircraft which made the first historic wireless flight between Biggin Hill and Paris. This one crashed on landing at the airfield.

Research to Defence

1923

AS Biggin Hill turned from research to defence so began another brilliant phase in the history of the station — this time as the headquarters of a Home Defence Squadron, the Anti-Aircraft School.

In 1923 the Army moved into the South Camp. Units representing the Anti-Aircraft School, the searchlight experimental establishment and the acoustical section took over the accommodation vacated by the IDE and worked in close co-operation with the RAF on the other camp.

Once established the three units began to make their presence felt. The school began to train personnel in the use of Anti-Aircraft guns, the searchlight unit developed improvements in the illumination of aircraft at night while the acoustical section undertook the vital task of obtaining early warning of an aircraft's approach.

The giant concrete disc left behind by the IDE was fitted with a bigger mirror for greater sensitivity and remained as a useful but hideous landmark until 1926 when it was demolished. Three aeroplanes had been written off after colliding with it.

A rare FE9 which crashed in the snow at Biggin Hill and broke in half in 1918, one of only three ever produced.

Peaceful days for the fighting 56

1923-27

No 56 fighter Squadron was one of the most renowned in the Royal Air Force and achieved considerable fame on the Western Front during the 1914-18 war.

Although this fighter squadron operated on The Bump in the peaceful, uneventful years of the mid-20's and was more involved in carrying out air exercises and co-operation on army manoeuvres than aerial combat, it was nonetheless involved in a series of dangerous escapades. One novel exercise was invented by the ground crew. The men would tie a bunch of hydrogen-filled balloons to their backs and hedge-hop across the fields in a series of gigantic leaps. L.A.C. Dodds, considered to be the champion hedge-hopper, fell to his death on the concrete apron outside the Guard Room when his balloon burst.

In 1924 the Squadron was re-equipped with the latest single-seater fighter the Gloster Grebe. On one occasion Flying Officer Luxmore, attempting to beat the Squadron record for consecutive loops ignored the Very signals ordering him to land, lost control and hit the ground in an explosion of flames. Five other pilots were killed in flying accidents during the four years 56 Squadron was at Biggin Hill.

In 1926 the Squadron took part in one of the great RAF pageants at Hendon. Joined by 54 fighters from five other squadrons it gave a brilliant display of aerobatics and earned the admiration of King George V.

A Sopwith IFI Camel of 'A' Flight, WEE which was used for pioneering wireless flights. This photograph was taken at Biggin Hill in 1918. (Photograph: RAF Museum)

The Night Flying Flight

1923-29

A Vickers Vimy biplane flown by Captain John Alcock from Britain and navigated by Lieutenant Arthur Whitten Brown landed on the Irish coast on June 15, 1919 after completing the first historic non-stop flight across the Atlantic. Four years later the Night Flying Flight was formed at Biggin Hill and equipped with three of these Rolls-Royce powered bombers with the knowledge that they were certainly capable of flying to Berlin and back and possibly further.

The Night Flying Flight was formed in July 1923 and had two main functions — to train pupils in night flying and to assist 56 Squadron and the Army School of Anti-Aircraft Defence in night attacks on heavy bombers. The fact that these giant Vimys were able to land with such frequency, day and night, on Biggin Hill's small grass airfield without mishap was one of the wonders of the time. There was, however, one fatality in the winter of 1924 during the making of a film re-enacting scenes of aerial combat. The circumstances were bizarre.

The director of the film company wanted a Vimy to be attacked and (apparently) shot down in flames by the fighters of 56 Squadron. The bomber was disguised for the occasion and as the fighters moved in for the attack, the rear gunner in the Vimy threw up his hands in mock agony and then pretended to be dead. The film makers continued to point their cameras at the bomber as it went into a steep dive with smoke rising from the engine and the fighters still in pursuit. Sadly, the pilot failed to pull out in time and crashed into a wood near Cudham. The film unit, unaware of the tragedy, believed the whole show was a brilliant touch of realism by the daredevil Vimy crew, until they were told that both occupants of the cockpit had been killed.

On May 5, 1926, the first general strike in British history began when the Trades Union Congress voted to back the miners in their dispute. Biggin Hill had an important role to play on behalf of the Government. All leave was cancelled and a cordon of armed sentries thrown around the station.

Each evening copies of the Government newspaper, the British Gazette were delivered by army lorries to Biggin Hill. The bundles were placed in the rear cockpit of the three Vimys which then took off on a long and unusual paper-round dropping copies of the Gazette over every town in the South.

Just before the general strike ended, a lorry carrying the newspapers was intercepted by a mob of strikers and overturned. That was the end of Biggin Hill's first and only aerial paper-round.

Corporal's dive to death

1927

IN the year that Charles Lindbergh became the first man to fly the Atlantic solo came the introduction of the parachute as standard equipment for the RAF. The young fighter pilots of 56 Squadron disliked this new safety aid but they took part enthusiastically in the basic training.

Lindbergh's success in being the first man across the Atlantic had galvanised public interest in the cause of aviation and made him a national hero overnight. His 3,600 mile flight was accomplished without a parachute.

A "Parachute Circus" toured the airfields with a Vickers Vimy and two small platforms were fitted around a strut on each wing. When it was airborne two parachutists climbed out of the cockpit, walked along the wing and stood on the strut. They were held upright by the pressure of the airstream and at a signal from the pilot they pulled the ripcord and jumped.

There was great excitement at Biggin Hill when the "Circus" arrived and the whole station turned out to watch. The parachutist Corporal East decided he would attempt to beat the world record for a delayed drop. He jumped from 6,000 feet but failed to release his parachute in time. He crashed onto the Bromley road just in front of a bus which had drawn up to allow the passengers to watch the display.

Shortly after, Lindbergh's son was kidnapped, held to ransom and then murdered. The famous aviator, in an attempt to escape public attention moved to Weald village near Sevenoaks. He may well have been a frequent visitor to Biggin Hill.

In the early 20's there were more than 200 members of the WRAF at Biggin Hill and many of them were recruited locally. Pictured here are Blanche Castle (left) and Christine Nelson who worked as typists in the Station office. (Photograph: John Nelson)

The power house staff of 1928. A feature of this photograph is that all the men are smoking pipes or cigarettes. It was fashionable at the time to puff as you posed — even in the power house!

Two Squadron Station *1932-36*

THE Salisbury Report of 1923 which recommended not only the retention of a separate air force but a measure of expansion, had a great influence on the future of Biggin Hill as a fighter station. It was proposed to introduce a second single-seater squadron there and provide more accommodation. The most economical solution was to demolish the temporary wooden huts, erected in 1917, and enlarge the North Camp.

Accordingly, 56 Squadron armed with Armstrong Whitworth Siskins, moved to North Weald leaving the Night Flying Flight as the only RAF unit at Biggin Hill and the builders free to go ahead with the ambitious expansion project.

Construction began in 1927 when 29 acres of land were purchased piecemeal from several owners. The airfield was extended, encompassing Cudham Lodge and all its property with suitable compensation for an unhappy John Westacott. By September 1932 the builders had finished, leaving North Camp with Messes for officers and NCO's, barrack blocks, married quarters and many other offices, all built in a red-brick style and typical of most RAF stations throughout England. These are the buildings which stand on the North Camp today, minus hangars and some offices, destroyed in the raids of 1940.

Meanwhile the Night Flying Flight remained behind to service the Anti-Aircraft School on the South Camp. Their work was absorbing and by the late 20's the unit had developed a system of huge acoustic concrete dishes and mirrors which were placed strategically along the south and east coasts. They were similar in appearance to radar dishes which superseded them. This concrete "ears and eyes" system can still be seen along the south Coast.

The station was reopened under the command of Wing Commander E.O. Grenfell and ready to become the home of two fighter Squadrons, 32 with Bristol Bulldogs and 23 with Bulldogs and Hawker Harts. The latter squadron was famous for its amazing displays of synchronised aerobatics at the Hendon Air Pageant and the Biggin Hill Show held on Empire Day. Sadly one of the squadron's most promising young officers, Douglas Bader suffered a crash just before his move to Biggin Hill and lost both his legs.

By October 1, 1932, 300 RAF personnel were occupying the North Camp. War clouds were not yet looming but the young pilots were encouraged to put in hundreds of hours flying. They played football and cricket at the station and became frequent visitors to the many nearby village pubs. Life at Biggin Hill in the early 30's was great fun.

Bristol Bulldogs of 32 Squadron. (Photograph: Imperial War Museum)

When Sir Alan Cobham's famous flying circus came to Biggin Hill one of the passengers was an 87-year old lady, Mrs Bath, believed at the time to be the oldest person to make a flight. Many fighter pilots of the second world war were given their first trip by Sir Alan including Wing Commander Ian Cosby DFC, who still lives in Biggin Hill. The aircraft is an Air Speed Ferry ABS1 AS4.

The Hawker Demons of 23 Squadron at Biggin Hill in June 1935. They became the only unit in the RAF to fly these two-seater fighters and gave some sensational displays of synchronised aerobatics at the Hendon Air Pageant. (Photograph: Quadrant Picture Library)

In common with other operational RAF stations Biggin Hill opened its gates to the public on Empire Day. This is the crowd which gathered in 1934 to witness an exhilarating display of aerobatics by the pilots of 32 and 23 Squadrons.

Home Defence Force

1936

THE Royal Air Force pageant at Hendon continued to be the highlight of the aeronautical year for the young pilots of 32 and 23 Squadrons and Biggin Hill ensured that they were always at their maximum efficiency for this prestige event.

The year 1935 brought alarming changes in the political situation of Europe and to the life style of squadrons at Biggin Hill. In October, Mussolini and his Fascists invaded Abyssinia. The Demons of 23 Squadron were dismantled and shipped out to the Middle East and a large section of the Squadron went with them as part of strategic reserves in case hostilities should spread. 32 Squadron remained at full strength, re-equipped with the new Gloster Gauntlets and for more than a year was Biggin Hill's only operational unit.

Meanwhile the situation at home was changing rapidly and by 1936 the nation became fully aware that war was a real possibility. 32 Squadron, brimming with confidence and highly proficient in Radio Telephony, was ready for action.

It was in 1936 that Adolf Hitler introduced his new fully fledged air force, the Luftwaffe, and people began to take notice of the warnings of Winston Churchill. Germany was known to be building modern bombers and a fair but alarming assumption at that time was that "the bomber will always get through".

In May 1936 Great Britain unveiled its drastically re-organised Home Defence Force which was given four functional commands — Bomber, Fighter, Coastal and Training. Biggin Hill came under Fighter Command and its headquarters were opened at Bentley Priory in July with Air Chief Marshal , Sir Hugh Dowding as AOC. Radar, or Radio Direction Finding (RDF) as it was then called was progressing and aircraft were being tracked at 40 miles range. In the autumn of 1936 Dowding chose Biggin Hill with its pioneering experience of ground-to-air and air-to-air contact in the 1914-18 war as the station to expand the theory and potential of this new weapon of defence.

The pilots of 32 Squadron worked unceasingly to perfect new techniques and procedures and in the Operations Room systems were developed using the simple "Principle of Equal Angles". This enabled controllers to plot invaders' exact positions and courses, and to direct fighters to intercept them.

In March 1937 "B" Flight was separated to form the nucleus of 79 Squadron. Additional pilots and machines were introduced and "Stuffy" Dowding made frequent visits to Biggin Hill to encourage both Squadrons.

Biggin Hill before the outbreak of the second world war. Above: the Anti Aircraft Defence School. Below: the RAF married quarters. (Photographs: John Nelson)

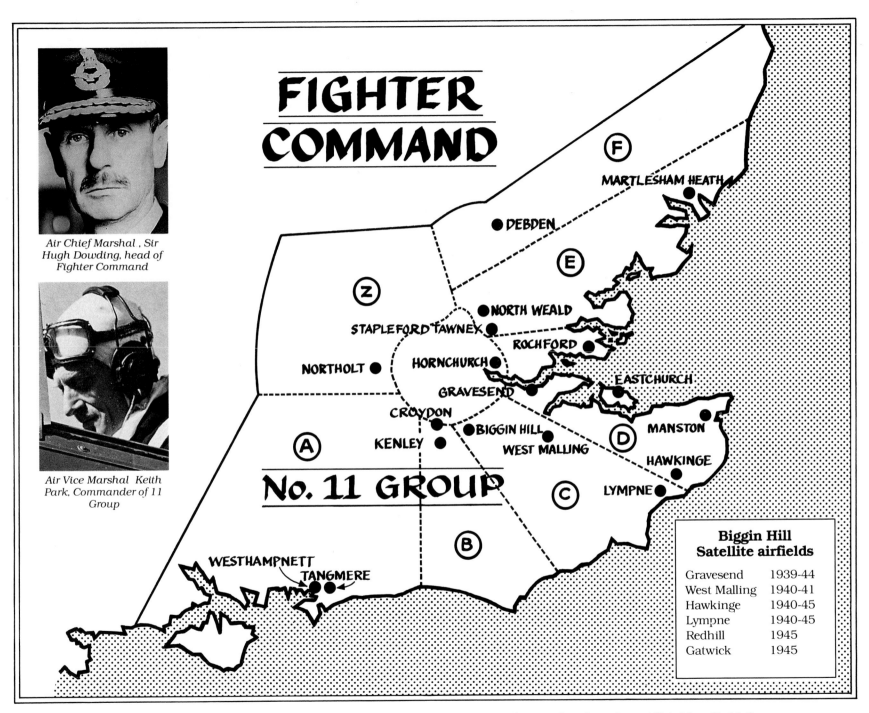

FIGHTER COMMAND

Air Chief Marshal , Sir Hugh Dowding, head of Fighter Command

Air Vice Marshal Keith Park, Commander of 11 Group

Ⓕ

MARTLESHAM HEATH

● DEBDEN

Ⓔ

Ⓩ

● NORTH WEALD

STAPLEFORD TAWNEY

ROCHFORD

NORTHOLT ●

HORNCHURCH

EASTCHURCH

GRAVESEND

CROYDON

Ⓐ

BIGGIN HILL

KENLEY

WEST MALLING

Ⓓ   MANSTON

HAWKINGE

No. 11 GROUP

Ⓒ   LYMPNE

Ⓑ

WESTHAMPNETT

TANGMERE

Biggin Hill Satellite airfields

Gravesend	1939-44
West Malling	1940-41
Hawkinge	1940-45
Lympne	1940-45
Redhill	1945
Gatwick	1945

No 11 Group of Fighter Command in which Biggin Hill was a sector station, with group headquarters at Uxbridge. No 11 Group was given the responsibility of defending the front line counties in southern England.

Airfield camouflage did not deceive

THIS is a pre-war reconnaissance photograph taken from the German airline Lufthansa en route for Croydon, some six miles to the north-west. The airfield had been carefully camouflaged but to the sharp eyes of the Lufthansa photographer it was obviously a key operational area.

The station commander was concerned about the physical appearance of Biggin Hill and sent up a pilot to see how well it was disguised. He flew above Sevenoaks and from 3,000 feet, five miles away could clearly see the orange paint of the hangars.

Efforts were made to camouflage the airfield even more but the Lufthansa pilots were not deceived. Photographs were frequently taken. On occasions a Junkers Transport would fly over the airfield and, when bad weather gave the excuse, the pilot would come inquisitively low. Once he was forced to climb rapidly into the clouds when a signal mortar was discharged across his nose by the duty pilot of 32 Squadron.

The Lufthansa and the Luftwaffe reconnaissance photographs taken in 1939 and 1940 were recovered after the war in German archives.

Hurricane and Spitfire — two special visitors

1938-1939

THERE was a buzz of excitement at Biggin Hill's Empire Day Show in 1938 over the presence of two visitors, both destined to play an historic role in the future of this fighter station. One of them was guarded by armed sentries while the other made a brief but spectacular appearance.

The first visitor was a Hawker Hurricane, an aircraft which had made itself famous one month earlier by covering the 327 miles from Edinburgh to Northolt at an average speed of 408 miles per hour. The second was a Spitfire — the first and only one at that time — which staged a sensational overhead demonstration before moving on to five other shows.

As Biggin Hill's summer wore on with growing uncertainty over the future, the pilots of the two squadrons continued to improve. 79 Squadron had already made the first formation flight at night to be carried out in Fighter Command when nine Gauntlets met at 6,000 feet over Sevenoaks and flew over Essex, London and Surrey before returning to Biggin Hill.

The Munich appeasement of September 1938 brought the station to "immediate readiness for war" (code word Diabolo) and all aircraft were ordered to be camouflaged in drab green and brown. Each pilot tackled his own machine with paint and brush, obliterating the squadron crest. On August 11, Biggin Hill received its first Miles Magister, a low-wing monoplane trainer and five weeks later, on the day before Chamberlain met the German delegation at Godesberg, a single-seater Hawker Hurricane was delivered to 32 Squadron.

Chamberlain's announcement of "peace in our time" was ignored at Biggin Hill. Wing Commander Dick Grice DFC took over command of the station and the aerodrome was disguised by camouflage experts. Trees and shrubs were planted, windows reinforced, blast walls and sandbag reinforcements constructed, runways and aprons toned down with bitumen and Army Ack Ack and ground defence units moved in to give cover from attack.

By now 601 (County of London) Auxiliary Squadron was partly mobilised with a detachment of Hawker Hurricanes to join 32 and 79. As 1939 arrived Biggin Hill was prepared for war.

Sir Philip Sassoon, a Staff Officer with Lord Haig in the 1914-18 war, a friend of the Royal Family, a Member of Parliament and an enthusiastic aviator is pictured here at Biggin Hill where he was a frequent visitor. Sir Philip, who lived at Port Lympne, became Commanding Officer of 601 Squadron in 1929, but he died before the outbreak of war. His house in Port Lympne was frequently used by pilots as a luxury billet during their days at the forward bases in the summer of 1940.

Flying Officer Peter Brothers of 32 Squadron took this picture of Gloster Gauntlets over Biggin Hill in 1938. For many months before the Munich crisis the Gauntlet pilots would go through the routine of wheeling the aircraft out of the hangar and then lining them up on the tarmac, wing tip to wing tip. The Squadron would be airborne sometime after 9am for air attack practice, air firing or interception of other aircraft. On rare occasions they flew twice in the morning and once in the afternoon, but the latter period was mostly spent servicing the Gauntlets. The Squadron was re-equipped with Hurricanes as the Munich crisis began to brew. Then the pilot's orderly life was replaced by a "high state of readiness" and they slept on bunks next to lockers containing their flying clothes.

Hurricane 1's of No 79 Squadron 'B' Flight in front of the North Camp triple-bay Belfast hangar in 1939. (Photograph: RAF Biggin Hill)

The Night that Churchill called in

September 1939

IN order to observe the effectiveness of a trial blackout in London, early in August, 1939, a young pilot from Biggin Hill was instructed to circle in a Hurricane over the capital and report the results on his R/T. Flying Officer Olding took off on a wild and stormy night, circled overhead once and then veered off towards Tatsfield. Seconds later there was a loud explosion. A second pilot, Flying Officer Wollaston, intending to drop a marker flare near the scene of the crash, also took off and, to the horror of those watching from outside the Mess, crashed into the top of Tatsfield Hill. The bodies of the men and the wrecked Hurricanes were found barely 100 yards apart.

Biggin Hill had lost two pilots and two Hurricanes, a tragedy that was to have even greater significance on August 24 when the station was instructed to mobilise and everyone on leave ordered to

return immediately. On the eve of war, 601 Squadron moved permanently from Hendon with Blenheims, temporarily adapted as fighters by the addition of a box of four Browning machine guns under the bomb bays. Now there were three fighter squadrons at Biggin Hill.

As the entire London balloon barrage went up on the evening of Saturday September 2, an old friend dropped into the Officers' Mess to give a few words of encouragement to the young pilots and ground crew. Winston Churchill was on his way home to Chartwell at Westerham. For years he had opposed Chamberlain's policy of appeasement and had frequently said that only a strong British air force could protect Britain from invasion. Giving nothing away about the enormous German superiority in air power, Churchill spoke to the young officers. "I've no doubt that you will be as brave and eager to defend your country as were your forefathers".

He then drove to Chartwell. At 11am the next morning, Sunday, Neville Chamberlain's voice came over the wireless. "I am speaking to you from the Cabinet Room of No 10 Downing Street . . . .".

3. WAR WITH GERMANY

September 1939

OFFICERS, Erks, WAAFS, Groundcrew, Controllers and Pilots of 32, 79 and 601 Squadrons listened to Chamberlain's broadcast on Sunday morning of September 3, 1939 and then, over the tannoy, heard the confirmation from their Station Commander: "As you will all have heard we are now at war with the Hun . . . .".

Wing Commander Grice's words were drowned by the immediate wailing of the sirens. Across London and the south-east thousands of people looked up at the sky for a sign of the bombers. The balloons rose around the capital and there was a dash to the nearest air-raid shelter.

At Biggin Hill, 32 Squadron was on "readiness". A telephone rang in their dispersal. "Blue Section, patrol Gravesend". An unidentified aircraft was coming up the Channel.

A few minutes later a French transport aircraft landed at Croydon, the pilot oblivious to the fact that he tested Fighter Command's complex defence system and had almost been blown out of the skies by 32 Squadron!

Later that day there was further excitement. Maidstone Searchlight Control reported that sound detectors were picking up enemy aircraft. Anti-aircraft batteries were alerted and 601 Squadron was scrambled. It was another false alarm. The ultra-sensitive detectors had picked up the electric motor of a fridge. The door had been left open.

Although all three squadrons put in many flying hours and some vigorous training exercises many weeks of boredom were to follow. The Luftwaffe's promised onslaught failed to arrive. The "Twilight War", as it was to be called, gave the station commander the opportunity to improve Biggin Hill's defences while the pilots chased occasional breakaway barrage balloons. On the South camp the 90th AA Regiment moved its guns closer and the army provided 75 privates to guard the airfield.

One defence measure taken during those September days of 1939 was the closure of the road between Bromley and Westerham to all private cars and pedestrians.

Local residents were to become accustomed to boarding a single decker bus with blacked out windows and proceeding across the airfield with an armed guard. If they were going towards Westerham they would be picked up at the Kings Arms, Leaves Green and deposited at The Black Horse and vice versa if travelling the other way. Motorists were required to make a huge detour to avoid the airfield.

Millionaire's Mob

Before the war the Auxiliary Air Force (AAF) was known for attracting aristocratic young men with a passion for weekend flying and a habit of disturbing the traditional peace of a British Sunday. The County of London 601 Squadron, was certainly in this mould but there was a serious purpose behind their play. The young pilots were keen to prove that, as amateurs, they could be the equal in combat to any regular RAF pilot — given the opportunity.

Max Aitken

When 601 flew in to make Biggin Hill its wartime base the rich, young pilots had little regard for the rigid discipline of the regular service. Among them was the Squadron Leader, Brian Thynne, Whitney Straight, Loel Guinness, Willy Rhodes-Moorhouse, Tom Hubbard, Roger Bushell, Sir Archibald Hope and Michael Peacock. They were immediately regarded as rivals by 32 Squadron who challenged them to a game of polo on old motor cycles. The boys of 601, using a stable of brand new Brough Superiors, easily won their first battle at "The Bump".

"The Millionaire's Mob", as they were dubbed, wore blue ties rather than black and lined their tunics with bright red silk. Almost every pilot owned his own private aircraft and among the best was an Aeronca G-ADZZ high wing monoplane belonging to John William Maxwell Aitken. Max was the son of "The Beaver", Lord Beaverbrook, the dynamic owner of the Daily Express and the Minister in charge of Aircraft Production.

Equipped with its Bristol Blenheim 1F converted fighters, 601 Squadron was in action on the day war was declared when 12 pilots were alerted to intercept the "intruder" over Knole Park — the motor of the refrigerator. As the Blenheims returned to Biggin Hill they suffered a further indignity. They were fired at by the anti-aircraft battery.

As with all his colleagues in 601 Squadron, Max Aitken became a distinguished fighter pilot, with many kills and a bag of honours. He had one unique record. On May 8, 1945, the day the European War officially ended, Max Aitken flew on an anti-shipping patrol near Aalborg, Denmark. He therefore flew on the first and last day of the war.

Group Captain Grice at Biggin Hill with King George VI.
(Photograph: RAF Biggin Hill)

Now he's 'Groupie'

September 1939

RICHARD Grice, who took over as Station Commander in December 1938, was the man who was to lead and inspire RAF Biggin Hill throughout the Battle of Britain. "Dickie", later to be called "Groupie", won the DFC during the 1914-18 war and accepted his duties at "The Bump" with all the enthusiasm and vigour of a first rate fighter pilot.

Shortly after war was declared in September 1939, Wing Commander Grice was promoted to Group Captain. This popular appointment called for a round of drinks at the White Hart, a splendid Tudor-style hotel eight miles down the road and his favourite place for relaxation.

Before he left for Brasted, the pilots placed the pipe-smoking Group Captain in an Armadillo vehicle and drove him round the dispersals at Biggin Hill. Pilots and ground crew alike applauded their station commander in his new senior role.

33

79 draws blood

November 21, 1939

AS Biggin Hill settled into the "Phoney War" of the winter of 1939/40 with routine and uneventful patrols, news came through on October 30 that No 1 Squadron had drawn first blood by shooting down a Dornier 17. How long would Biggin have to wait before it joined the fray?

The answer was three more weeks. 79 Squadron, deployed briefly at Manston, broke the lull by making Biggin Hill's first kill on November 21, 1939. Two Hurricanes were ordered to patrol Hawkinge at 10am and for 20 minutes, in foul weather, they flew up and down the coast on what looked like another abortive mission.

At 10.20am the radio location operators spotted a blip on the screen. This one looked more menacing than usual. Could this be the Hun at last?

The Controller spoke to Flying Officer Jimmy Davies in the first Hurricane: "Hello, Pansy Yellow Leader. Sapper Control. Vector 115 degrees. Angels 15. Buster!" Pansy was the code name for 79 Squadron. Yellow leader was Davies. Sapper was the code name for Biggin Hill.

Davies, a young American, understood the message. So did Flight Sergeant Brown in the second Hurricane. Swinging onto the new course over the Channel, the pilots switched on their gun sights and looked for their prey — a Dornier 17 "flying pencil", obviously making a weather reconnaisance over the sea.

Davies was the first to dive, opening fire with his Browning guns 600 feet from his target. Brown followed and the Dornier spun onto its back and vanished into cloud. Davies and Brown chased it through the mist and saw pieces flying off in all directions. The Dornier hit the sea and exploded. Biggin Hill had joined the war.

Blenheim IF's of 601 Squadron. The nearest is piloted by Flight Lieutenant Roger Bushell who was shot down over Dunkirk and taken prisoner. Roger became "OC Escaping" in the notorious Stalag Luft III and was murdered by the Gestapo after a mass breakout in 1944. See picture page 116.

Mission at Borkum

November 29, 1939

Eight days after the first kill by Davies and Brown, Biggin Hill was involved in a dangerous and highly secret mission. Six Blenheim 1Fs of 601 Squadron were ordered to Northolt where the pilots joined up with another six 1Fs of 25 Squadron, and were then briefed. At dusk the following day the 12 Blenheims raided the Luftwaffe seaplane base at Borkum in the Friesian Islands after a 250-mile flight across the North Sea. None carried either a dinghy or even a life-preserver jacket.

Four sections of three Blenheims, two led by Flying Officers Michael Peacock and Max Aitken dived out of the clouds and, from 100 feet, strafed the slipways, hangars, ships and machine gun posts with bullets. Within five minutes it was all over. Five seaplanes were wrecked, patrol boats sunk and gunners lay dead by their posts. The raiding Blenheims returned without a scratch.

Michael Peacock was awarded the DFC for his action in this, the first RAF fighter foray against German territory. The other four pilots who flew on this mission were Flight Lieutenant Tom Hubbard, Flight Lieutenant Sir Archibald Hope, Flying Officers Carl Davis and Willy Rhodes-Moorhouse.

In September 1940, Davis, flying a Hurricane, was shot down and killed, his aircraft crashing into a garden at Matfield. Rhodes-Moorhouse died on the same day when his Hurricane plunged into High Brooms Viaduct, near Tunbridge Wells.

Hurricane weather

January to May 1940

'I can only think that the Boche is waiting for fine weather. Otherwise he could come through us and the French like a hot knife through butter. Well come along Grice, show me your anti-aircraft defences and remember you're protecting my house as well as the aerodrome '.

Churchill at Biggin Hill early in 1940

AS New Year 1940 dawned, Biggin Hill looked more like a building site than a fighter station. All three squadrons were on deployment elsewhere while workmen laid a short but substantial runway and excavated deep air-raid shelters. Occasionally a Luftwaffe reconnaissance aircraft would fly over and the pessimistic view was that bombs would be hitting the newly-laid runway before the concrete had dried.

The winter of 1940 was severe. Blizzards and deep snow made flying impossible. The construction gangs, however, completed their work and by April, 32 and 79 Squadrons had returned to "The Bump". 601 Squadron remained at Tangmere.

Squadron Leader John "The Baron" Worrall took over as Officer in Command of 32 Squadron on May 6 and, within a week, was leading 12 Hurricanes across the Channel towards The Hague. His orders were to strafe Ypenburg aerodrome, reputedly in German hands.

When the Hurricanes reached Ypenburg they saw no opposition but hundreds of discarded parachutes. Below were the burnt-out wrecks of 16 Junkers 52s. One troop carrier remained intact. The aircraft, now beyond radio transmission range and unable to hear the order to abandon the mission, swept over the airfield spraying bullets into hangars and destroying the lone Junkers.

Satisfied with their work but puzzled by the lack of opposition, they returned to Biggin Hill to learn that Dutch patriots had earlier recaptured Ypenburg and shot up every troop carrier but one. That was to be used for the escape to England!

A few days later 11 Hurricanes of 32 Squadron came face to face with nine Me109s escorting a Dornier bomber. "Red Knight" Crossley, Pete Brothers and "Jack" Daw each claimed a 109 while Sergeant White sent the Dornier spiralling dramatically to earth. In this hectic battle Daw got hopelessly lost and checked his gyro compass. He had been flying due east for 20 minutes and was on course for Berlin. Turning round the pilot made it back to Biggin Hill with just enough fuel for a victory roll!

Scramble! Pilots of 32 Squadron race to their Mk 1 Hurricanes against the background of the Belfast type hangar. (Photograph: Kent Messenger)

A postcard from Millie

May 19, 1940

THE first pilot of the "32nd Pursuit" to be lost in action was Flying Officer Milner who was engaged with 10 colleagues in the hectic dog-fight over France on May 19, 1940. "Millie the Moocher", as he was known, was the only Hurricane pilot who failed to return to Biggin Hill after the action. His fellow officers were distressed.

Many weeks later the Squadron received this message on a postcard from a Kriegsgefangenenlager: "Sorry I left you the other day. I wasn't thinking. Wonder if you are still at "The Bump". Do drop in and see me any time you're around these parts. Love to everyone and good luck. Millie."

On May 10, 1940, the day that Hitler invaded the Low Countries, there was an event of some significance as far as Biggin Hill was concerned. The first Spitfires to fly from "The Bump" arrived with 610 (County of Chester) Squadron, who took over the quarters vacated that day by 79 Squadron who were dispatched to Merville in France. Led by Squadron Leader A.L. Franks, 610 joined the "32nd Pursuit", the Squadron which had fathered them in 1937. The Spitfire Mark II having its machine guns test fired belongs to 72 Squadron who arrived later in the summer of 1940. (Photograph: Imperial War Museum)

On May 10, 1940, 79 Squadron arrived at Merville and our picture shows four young pilot officers in earnest discussion with a French pilot and crew. 79 Squadron returned to Biggin Hill as evacuees after severe fighting. They claimed 25 enemy aircraft but lost many pilots and most of their Hurricanes, which were left at Merville bombed and burnt out. Left to right: Pilot Officer Lou Appleton, killed four days later, Pilot Officer J.E.R. Wood, killed July 8, Pilot Officer Donald (Dimsy) Stones and in the centre Pilot Officer Jimmy Davies, killed on June 27. (Photograph: RAF Biggin Hill)

Operation Dynamo

May 27-June 5, 1940

'By the end of the first week of Dunkirk air fighting had gone from 7,000 feet to more that 20,000. The Germans did this and we did that. We did that and the Germans did this. Air fighting moved from a low level right up, high in the sky.' H.M. Stephen — 74 Squadron.

BIGGIN Hill played a vital role in "Operation Dynamo", the great evacuation of Dunkirk, but the responsibility to provide part of the air cover while the expeditionary forces were rescued from the beaches did not fall on the weary shoulders of the pilots of 32 or 79 Squadrons. The men who had been in constant action since early May were sent away for a well-deserved rest.

The two new squadrons to "The Bump" were 213 and 242 and they went immediately into action. On Day One of the Operation the Hurricanes were on a joint patrol over Gravelines when they met ten Me109s and shot down two without loss. On the second day, 213 Squadron found itself hopelessly outnumbered by Junkers 88s and Heinkel 111s covered by 109s. They were dropping bombs on beaches swarming with troops but in a battle lasting just five minutes seven German aircraft were shot down and several damaged. One Hurricane pilot, Pilot Officer Stone, was killed.

Day after day the struggle continued. 610 Squadron had eight kills and four probables but they lost six Spitfires — half of their Squadron. On June 4 they were pulled out of the action to rest at Gravesend. Their replacement was 229 who came in with Hurricanes from Digby on May 25.

By the end of the first week of June "Dynamo" was over. More than 338,000 British and Allied troops had been snatched from defeat by the Royal Navy and a flotilla of little boats. The Hurricanes from Biggin Hill had played their part by constantly patrolling the skies and keeping the Luftwaffe at bay. In nine days of fighting the station had accounted for 36 German aircraft with 20 probables.

The cost had been high. Through the retreat the Army lost 68,000 men killed, missing, or taken prisoner. A total of 243 ships were sunk. The RAF lost 474 aircraft. Biggin Hill earned its first Battle Honour but lost eight pilots, eight Hurricanes and six Spitfires.

The tempo and intensity of Luftwaffe raids continued. There was no respite.

The crowded deck of a troopship as officers and other ranks of the RAF are rescued from Dunkirk. (Photograph: Imperial War Museum)

4. BATTLE OF BRITAIN

‘ What General Weygand called the Battle of France is over. I expect the Battle of Britain is about to begin. Upon this battle depends the survival of Christian civilisation. Upon it depends our own British life and the long continuity of our institutions and our Empire. The whole fury and might of the enemy must very soon be turned on us. Hitler knows that he will have to break us in this island or lose the war. If we can stand up to him, all Europe may be free and the life of the world may move forward into broad, sunlit uplands. But if we fail, then the whole world, including the United States, including all that we have known and cared for, will sink into the abyss of a new Dark Age, made more sinister and perhaps more protracted, by the lights of perverted science. Let us therefore brace ourselves to our duties, and so bear ourselves that, if the British Empire and its Commonwealth last for a thousand years, men will still say: This was their finest hour ’.

Winston S. Churchill, June 1940

Fall of France

June 1940

BY mid-June, 1940 the Nazi swastika was flying from the Eiffel Tower and the Arc de Triomphe. The French had surrendered and Hitler was in Paris to relish their humiliation. Now he had control of Continental Europe and, after the retreat of Dunkirk, the British Army was in total disarray. The tempting islands of Britain were his for the taking, just a few miles across a narrow stretch of water.

At Biggin Hill the weather was delightfully warm and the station with its new runway, air-raid shelters and many new trees and shrubs was in perfect trim. The reinforcement squadrons of 213 and 242, having completed their duty at Dunkirk, had departed and 32 and 79 Squadrons (father and son) were back with the necessary reserve to cope with the stresses and strains of the weeks ahead. The young pilots knew that Hitler was wasting no time in putting together an invasion fleet in preparation for a massive landing.

The Hurricanes of Biggin Hill were constantly in action, escorting Blenheims on bombing raids and meeting Me109s in the hot, cloudless skies. On June 7 and 8 the two squadrons shared a bag of 14 with four probables. No losses to 79 but three pilots of 32 Squadron were missing, including 20-year-old "Grubby" Grice, DFC, who had been with the Squadron since the days of peace. Three days later Mike Crossley wrote in his squadron diary: "Grubby returns. Heil Grubby".

In July Reichsmarschall Hermann Goering ordered his bombers to attack British ships and lure the aircraft of Fighter Command into new battles over the Channel. He believed the British were short of trained pilots and machines and would lose even more in long-range sorties.

Britain was short of pilots but every day more Allied airmen from Occupied France were being recruited at fighter stations across England. The output of aircraft was also rising steadily; Hurricanes, Spitfires and bombers. Britain had calculated that the Germans would need at least 250 vessels to transport a force of about 100,000 men across the Channel. The most likely landing places were in an arc of Kent and Sussex between Dover and Brighton. Defending that part of England was No 11 Group of Fighter Command and Biggin Hill was a senior sector station.

The Luftwaffe were now operating out of French airfields. They had more than 3,500 aircraft on 400 airfields. All Hitler needed to do was wipe the Royal Air Force from the skies before the onset of winter. The Battle of Britain was about to begin.

When war was declared an appeal for recruits for the Women's Auxiliary Air Force was broadcast by the BBC and from all walks of life hundreds of women immediately volunteered. Biggin Hill welcomed its first recruits during the autumn of 1939 but could offer little in the way of adequate accommodation or training. The few WAAFs at the station had to contend with difficult, makeshift conditions and, sadly, prejudice from some of the men who felt that women had no part to play in the service. However, the spirit of the girls was amazing and they set about their daily tasks as cooks, drivers, equipment assistants, clerks or orderlies with an energy and willingness that made even the most sceptical think again. The WAAFs brought to Biggin Hill a family atmosphere of care and concern and by mid-summer of 1940 there were more than 250 girls serving alongside the RAF. Photograph shows some of the WAAFs. They include Sergeant Helen Turner (left), and Sergeant Elizabeth Mortimer.

King at Biggin Hill

June 27, 1940

During their days of defensive patrols and scrambles, the pilots often used the forward stations of Hawkinge, Lympne and Manston. They would fly to other Kent airfields at dawn, returning to Biggin Hill at night. It was exhausting and eventful.

On June 27, 1940, 79 Squadron took off from Manston to escort a flight of Blenheims on a photographic reconnaissance and on the way back met three 109s, diving out of the sun. In the fight that ensued the Hurricanes of Pilot Officer Davies and Sergeant McQueen went down in flames. McQueen baled out over the Channel and was seen floating on his back in the sea. The Rye lifeboat found McQueen dead.

Later that day, King George VI came to Biggin Hill to honour those officers who had distinguished themselves in the Dunkirk and French campaigns. There were Distinguished Flying Crosses for Michael Crossley, "Jack" Daw, "Grubby" Grice of 32 Squadron and Jimmy Davies and "Dimsy" Stones of 79 Squadron. Sergeants Whitby and Cartwright of 79 Squadron had won the Distinguished Flying Medal.

It was a poignant ceremony. At the end of the day a DFC lay uncollected. The American, Jimmy Davies, was missing. He was the second Hurricane pilot to die that day.

Flight Lieutenant Crossley receives his DFC while Pilot Officers Daw, Grice, Stones and Sergeants Whitby and Cartwright await their turn.

HQ officers in 1940

Station HQ staff at Biggin Hill in 1940. Officers in the top row include: Flight Lieutenant Stone, Flying Officer Smith, Flying Officer Paxton, Pilot Officer Yorke, Flight Lieutenant Osmond and Pilot Officer Leeming. Front row (left to right): Flight Lieutenant Deans, Flight Lieutenant Jackson .....?....., Squadron Leader Moody (Station Adjutant), Group Captain Grice (Station Commander), Flight Lieutenant Russell, Flight Lieutenant Baker, Squadron Leaders Holt and Curwood. (Photograph: David Porter)

A vital part of the air battles of 1940 was the work of the ground crews in re-arming the aircraft (see picture). Another was the conversion of all aircraft to constant speed propellers. When engineers from the de Havilland Company arrived at Biggin Hill on June 26 to complete this task they found that the Spitfires were still at Gravesend with 610 Squadron. Rather than tackle the Hurricanes first, the team spent several days at Gravesend and were delighted to be the first in the country to put an operational constant speed Spitfire into the air. Then they converted the Hurricanes of Biggin Hill. In a week the job was done, the new units giving the aircraft a better rate of climb, a higher ceiling and a faster power dive. They were now superior to the Me109.
(Photograph: Imperial War Museum)

Slaughter of the Innocents

July 19, 1940

A tragic chapter in the history of Biggin Hill began on July 12, 1940 when Squadron Leader W.A. Richardson brought 141 Squadron south from Turnhouse, near Edinburgh with 12 Boulton Paul Defiant two-seat fighters. The Squadron established its headquarters in the South Camp of Biggin Hill although the aircraft were to operate from West Malling.

The Defiant had introduced a new tactical concept in two seat fighters whereby no forward firing guns were fitted. All offensive power was concentrated in the rear cockpit by a four gun power-operated turret. 264 Squadron had taken the Defiant into battle on May 12, 1940 with splendid results. On the 29th of that month the Squadron destroyed 37 enemy aircraft in one operation, the Germans mistakenly identifying the Defiants as Hurricanes and diving on their supposedly defenceless tails. By May 31, Defiants had shot down 65 enemy aircraft and were thus dubbed infallible.

The squadron was ready for operations by July 18 and the first scramble came the next day when the 12 Defiants flew to the forward airfield at Hawkinge. By mid-day they were at readiness and were airborne at 12.32pm when only nine of the Defiants took off. Engine trouble kept two on the ground whilst the third could not complete his take-off run.

141 was assigned to patrol a line south of Folkestone at a height of 5,000 feet, reaching this just as the sirens around the area began to sound. The Luftwaffe were bombing Dover Harbour escorted by a force of 20 Messerschmitt 109's of the second Gruppe of Jagdgeschwader 51 operating from St Omer. Given a new course, 141 was vectored to a point off Cap Gris Nez when Flight Lieutenant Loudon in Defiant L7001 saw the 109's diving out of the sun. Flying in sections of three, line astern, the Defiants opened out to bring their guns round to deliver a beam attack. Unfortunately, since the last contact with the Defiants, the German pilots had realised the most vulnerable spot on this aircraft was its belly. The 109's, therefore, dived past the Defiants and came up underneath them where they knew the power-operated turret could not bear down on them.

In seconds, two Defiants were going down in flames into the sea. Pilot Officer J.R. Kemp with his gunner Sergeant R. Crombie and Pilot Officer R.A. Howley with Sergeant A.G. Curley were not seen again. Minutes later Pilot Officer R. Kidson and Sergeant F.P.J. Atkins were also lost at sea. The slaughter continued as a fourth Defiant was hit. Pilot Officer J.R. Gardner, although wounded, managed to bale out before the aircraft hit the sea. His gunner, Pilot Officer D.M. Slater was lost.

With 141 trying desperately to fire at the 109's, the German pilots regrouped for a second attack as a fifth Defiant with Flight Lieutenant M.J. Loudon and Pilot Officer E. Farnes was hit in the engine. Managing to evade his aggressor and although wounded in the arm, Loudon told his gunner to abandon the aircraft as he attempted to reach Hawkinge. He crashed short of the airfield but lived. His gunner also survived having been picked up by a launch of the Air Sea Rescue.

The carnage continued when a sixth Defiant crashed at Elmsvale Road, Dover. Flight Lieutenant I.D.G. Donald DFC and Pilot Officer A.C. Hamilton were killed outright as the 7th aircraft, although badly hit, managed to crash-land at Hawkinge. Tragically, the pilot, Pilot Officer I.M. McDougall had advised his gunner, Sergeant J.F. Wise, to bale out when the aircraft lost power after it was hit. Although the engine was emitting black smoke and glycol was streaming out, it picked up sufficiently for McDougall to attempt to make Hawkinge. After seeing that his gunner was swimming strongly towards the shore, he headed for the airfield. Sergeant Wise was never seen again.

Only two intact Defiants returned to Hawkinge and they themselves may not have made it but for the timely intervention of 111 Squadron with their Hurricanes. For the Luftwaffe it was a triumph even though one 109, flown by Feldwebel Heilmann and damaged by a 141 Defiant, crashed on return to St Omer killing the pilot.

For 141 Squadron, its first action of the war had ended in tragedy with six aircraft lost, four pilots and five gunners killed. The rest of the Squadron were released from operations and were posted back to Prestwick for conversion to night-fighting duties.

At Biggin Hill, the rumour had got around that the entire Squadron had been wiped out. It was later confirmed that two intact aircraft and one damaged had made Hawkinge. The day became known as the slaughter of the innocents.

Robin Brooks

In July 1940 32 Squadron welcomed three Polish airmen to "The Bump". Pilot Officers, Pfeiffer, Wlasnowalski and Pniak, better known as Fifi, Vodka and Cognac! First they were given a conversion course on Hurricanes under the watchful eye of training officer "Polly" Flinders. On his first solo Wlasnowalski struck the boundary fence, cartwheeled over the main road and landed right way up in a back garden. His compatriot Pniak found him unhurt but admonished him severely for disgracing Poland! The picture above was taken by Peter Brothers of the "32nd Pursuit". Standing: Pfeiffer, Humpherson, Gardener, Crossley, Grice, Pain. Seated: Eckford, Pniak and Wlasnowalski.

Farewell to Friends

July, 1940

THE long daylight hours of July saw 32 and 610 Squadrons continuing with relentless scrambles and patrols from Hawkinge, "Hellfire Corner". They would often start their day at 5am and finish at 8.30pm, flying three, sometimes four, sorties a day.

The casual pictures of pilots lying on the ground, lounging in deck chairs or playing cards in the sunshine belies the real tension of those hours waiting for a scramble. The atmosphere at the dispersal was often electric and tempers would frequently flare. On occasions a pilot would disappear behind the hut to retch and heave but when the real thing came he would sprint furiously to his aircraft, clip on his parachute and climb into the cockpit. Both 32 and 610 could be airborne in two minutes.

On July 10, the Spitfire flown by "Big Bill" Smith, a large likeable Liverpudlian who was Commanding Officer of 610 Squadron, was hit in the port mainplane by an Me109 during combat over Dover. He crash-landed at Hawkinge and was miraculously unhurt.

Two days later 610 Squadron lost Sergeant Ireland when he dived out of control during dogfight practice and crashed into Titsey Park, near Westerham. On July 13, Sergeant Watson-Parker failed to return from a routine patrol. On the 18th, Pilot Officer Litchfield was shot down and killed over the Channel.

Smith, who had taken over as Commanding Officer when Squadron Leader Franks died at Dunkirk, was concerned by the growing list of casualties. But his own life was to be short. On July 25 his Spitfire was hit again on a patrol over Dover and Smith braced himself for another crash-landing at Hawkinge. As he approached the runway the Spitfire stalled, dived into a disused engine testing shed and burst into flames.

John Ellis was now temporarily in charge and on the same day led seven Spitfires into combat against 20 Me109s and bombers which were attacking a destroyer. Breaking up, the Spitfires took it in turns to fly directly at the enemy and from a few yards range empty their ammunition. Ellis's target rolled over and crashed into the sea, followed by another 109. Five minutes later a third Messerschmitt crashed into the Channel near Dover and a fourth came down at Elvington Court, near Deal. Three German pilots were killed and a fourth captured. There was no loss to 610 who had avenged the death of "Big Bill" in an action typical of the many fought out over the Channel from "Hellfire Corner".

During July, 27 Junkers and Me109s were shot down by the Biggin Hill squadrons but the Luftwaffe kept on coming. Indeed its attacks intensified, for it was still only using a fraction of its strength.

Sergeant Bill Neville had a tragically short career as a fighter pilot: the 26-year-old from Shepperton joined 610 Squadron on July 27, 1940 and on August 8 escaped from an overturned Spitfire at Wittersham. Three days later he was reported missing after a patrol over the Channel off Calais.

Twenty five British airmen lost their lives on August 11, 1940, the worst day for aircrew casualties during the Battle of Britain. Among them was Flight Sergeant John Tanner, aged 25, who also failed to return from a patrol over the Channel at 11.30am. Tanner, like his friend Bill Neville, had joined 610 Squadron in July.

Pilots of 610 Squadron at "Hellfire Corner", Hawkinge on the morning of July 29, 1940. Left to right (standing): Flying Officer Stan Norris, Sergeant Horatio Chandler, Squadron Leader John Ellis (just visible), Flight Lieutenant Bill Warner, Sergeant Ronnie Hamlyn, Pilot Officer Fred Gardiner and Flying Officer Doug Wilson. Left to right (on ground): Flight Lieutenant Edward Smith, Pilot Officer Joe Pegge (on his back), Sergeant Claude Parsons, Sergeant Doug Corfe. Of these pilots Warner was killed three weeks later, on August 16. Parsons died in 1941 and Corfe in 1942. On the day this photograph was taken Stan Norris's Spitfire was damaged in combat over the Channel but he returned safely to base at 1.15pm. (Photograph: RAF Biggin Hill)

The fourth platoon (F Coy) of the 20th Battalion at Biggin Hill. (Photograph: Bertie Miller)

The Home Guard

July 1940

WHEN the Secretary of State for War, Anthony Eden, appealed for volunteers to form a Local Defence Force, the public responded with tremendous enthusiasm. Patriots, too young or too old for active service, flocked to their local police station to enrol and were given arm bands, and a rapid briefing about their responsibilities should England be invaded.

Within six days of Mr Eden's broadcast the recruitment figure stood at 250,000. Many of them were veterans of the Great War "keen to do their bit again." They armed themselves with shotguns, cutlasses and even broomsticks converted into pikes. It was the first citizens army since Napoleon threatened to invade English soil in 1803.

The platoon assigned to look after Biggin Hill and the locality around the airfield was F Company of the 20th Battalion who elected Major Smithers of Knockholt as their Commanding Officer and Bertie Miller, a local builder, as Lieutenant. Both were veterans of the 1914-18 war. Like every LDV unit in the country, senior officers stood shoulder to shoulder with former privates while old men and schoolboys from all walks of life displayed their keenness to become part of an effective army.

In July, Winston Churchill suggested the LDV be renamed the Home Guard. Proper uniforms were issued and real weapons and military discipline introduced. The Fourth Platoon at Biggin Hill was rapidly reorganised and was soon guarding key installations and showing better than average accuracy in rifle practice.

Within a month this motley but disciplined band of men had gained national fame as the only unit of the Home Guard to bring down a German bomber. But was it true? Certainly wartime propaganda made them into instant heroes.

We're waiting for you, Jerry! Guns of the 90th AA Regiment, deployed around the aerodrome, are ready to burst into life.
(Photograph: RAF Biggin Hill)

The storm breaks

August 12, 1940

BIGGIN Hill was now aware of Hitler's plans. He aimed to put every radar station between Portland and the Thames out of action and, simultaneously, attack coastal shipping and all the airfields. The Spitfires of 610 and the Hurricanes of 32 were among those who were going to try and stop him. This was August 12 and a "blitzy" morning lay ahead.

It was some time before the telephone rang in 610's dispersal but at 7.31 the order came through. "Squadron Scramble. Dungeness. 10,000 feet". Within seconds the Merlin engines roared into life, the Spitfires of 610 took off and Ellis was reporting his position back to Biggin Hill Control. The answer came back immediately. "Thankyou, Dog Rose Red Leader. Receiving you loud and clear. Vector 120 degrees. Nine bandits approaching Dungeness Angels 10. Good hunting".

Just under an hour later the Spitfires of 610 Squadron began to straggle home. A victory roll from Red Leader Ellis. Another from Sergeant Bernard Gardner and two more from Pilot Officers Constantine Pegge and Ken Cox. Group Captain Grice, puffing his pipe, was waiting for them to return. So was "Spy" de le Torre, the Intelligence Officer who knew the lads had been involved in a big "show" over the Channel. He wanted to hear their reports. It was apparently a dog fight with nine Dornier 215s and a large escort of Me 109s. The score was uncertain. Two 109s were definitely destroyed with six unconfirmed, two "probables" and one damaged. Two Spitfire pilots were missing — Flying Officer Gardiner and Flight Lieutenant Smith.

A short time later the whole of Biggin Hill heard the sound of an injured Spitfire. It bounced heavily onto the runway, petrol leaking and the port aileron hanging limply. Fred Gardiner, wounded in the leg by exploding cannon shell, was helped out of his cockpit. "Smithy", he said, "has baled out over the Channel."

Ted Smith had an even luckier escape. His Spitfire was hit by shells, the engine stopped and flames burst out of the instrument panel. As the Spitfire dived towards the sea, Smith tugged on the hood but the force of the wind was holding it back. The young Flight Lieutenant, trying not to panic, blinded by smoke, pulled back the stick to reduce the speed of his Spitfire. He released the hood, took off his seat harness, tumbled out of the aircraft and pulled the ripcord. Moments later he was being rescued from the sea.

Great Stuff This R.A.F.!

(Courtesy of The National Newspaper Library)

32 against the world

August 12, 1940

THE young pilots of 610 Squadron, average age just under 21, had survived the first day of grouse shooting and happily renamed it "Hun shooting". The Luftwaffe, however, had achieved much of its first objective. Four radio location stations had been damaged, two convoys bombed and ships in Portsmouth Harbour were on fire. 32 Squadron were ordered to Hawkinge. Its adventures that day would start after lunch.

Hellfire Corner lived up to its name. While Squadron Leader Michael Crossley and his Hurricane pilots were pitting their skills against a massive formation of Dornier 17s and Me109s in a series of dogfights, incendiary bombs were raining down on Hawkinge aerodrome. Returning for fuel, Crossley and four other pilots saw the smoking hangars and cratered runways below. Over the R/T Crossley made his cool decision. "Hello, Sparrow (Hawkinge) Control. Jacko Red Leader calling. So sorry to trouble you. Afraid we simply must pancake".

"Hello Jacko Red Leader. We've had a spot of bother here", the Controller replied. "Permission to pancake granted. Good luck".

The devastation at Hawkinge was appalling, hangars, workshops and domestic buildings flattened and others burning. From the water tower sprang a series of fountains caused by bomb splinter holes and over the station lay a slowly drifting cloud of dust and smoke. Hawkinge was out of commission yet Crossley, with his fuel-less Hurricanes managed to land.

The Junkers 88s, having gone on to put Manston and Lympne out of action, returned to Hawkinge while mechanics were working on the grounded Hurricanes. Hobson's choice faced the pilots of 32 Squadron. They rushed to the air raid shelters and prayed that the Hurricanes would survive. They did. All five of them.

Returning to Biggin Hill, Crossley and friends gave their account of the battle. 90 Huns against 12 Hurricanes. 32 Squadron against the world! Eleven victims, their highest score to date. One casualty, Pilot Officer Barton shot down over Dover.

Tony Barton's Hurricane was destroyed but the Pilot Officer baled out and made his way back to Biggin Hill. His colleagues found him in the Mess, enjoying a beer. Next day he was shot down again, making a forced landing.

While pilots at Biggin Hill relaxed, everyone at Hawkinge and Manston was working through the night. With massive help from the Army the two aerodromes were operational by dawn on August 13, as were all but one of the radar stations.

THE RED KNIGHT

WHEN Michael Crossley, commander of 32 Squadron, first heard Churchill's immortal words 'never . . . . has so much been owed by so many . . . .', he said to his boys: "Be careful, chaps, the Prime Minister has seen our Mess Bill"!

From the diary of Michael Crossley. **August 15, 1940 (Thursday)**. *Down to Hawkinge 1pm and from then on had a remarkably blitzy afternoon. Chased something up to Harwich and got mixed up with 109s going home. Got none. They got "Grubby" (Grice) instead. Back to Biggin, refuel, off to Portsmouth and attacked thousands of 17s who were beating up and bombing Croydon. Slapped down seven.*

A message from Goering

"From Reichsmarschall Goering to all units of Air Fleets 2, 3 and 5. Operation Eagle. Within a short period you will wipe the British Air Force from the sky. Heil Hitler".

The next day was Adlertag — August 13, 1940 — the day when Goering was to crush the RAF and clear the way for "Sealion".

For two days the skies were overcast. The assault came on August 15.

Party at Croydon

August 15

THURSDAY August 15 is a day that will always be associated with Biggin Hill and the Battle of Britain. It was the day the Luftwaffe sent over 1,800 aircraft in five massive assaults with the intention of putting every airfield out of action. It was the day the RAF scrambled its greatest ever number of fighters to meet a single enemy operation — some 150 Hurricanes and Spitfires right across Southern England.

During this memorable Thursday, all 21 of 11 Group squadrons were in action and some, like 32 Squadron, were scrambled three times. Against these massive odds the RAF lost 34 fighters and shot down 182 enemy aircraft, a figure that may have been highly exaggerated due to confusing reports but certainly one that gave an indication of the scale of the day's fighting.

Priority airfields for the bombers were Kenley and Biggin Hill. By mistake Croydon airfield was hit instead of Kenley — a raid that came with appalling suddenness for bombs were falling as the sirens were wailing. The Dorniers also missed Biggin Hill and dropped bombs on the incomplete grass airfield of West Malling, killing two airmen. Over northern Kent the massed Dorniers damaged the Short Brothers aircraft works in Rochester, whose final assembly line was producing, not fighters, but Britain's first four-engined bombers, the massive Stirling.

The two Biggin Hill squadrons were on readiness from first light but it was not until the early afternoon that 32 Squadron was sent to Harwich to intercept some Me109s streaking back across the sea. The Germans, low on fuel, were in no mood for a fight but one pilot turned aggressively and fired an accurate burst at "Grubby" Grice. His Hurricane fell from the sky in a blazing inferno.

610 Squadron was not out of the action. Flight Lieutenant Warner leading eight Spitfires met a formation of Dornier 17s and their escorting Me109s heading towards Biggin Hill. They sent two bombers plunging to earth and attacked the Messerschmitts so aggressively that they turned and fled. While this was going on a second formation of Dorniers sneaked through to Croydon. 32 Squadron could see the smoke rising and according to their squadron diary "we turned and beat it to Croydon as fast as we could. Sure enough we saw a large party in progress. Masses of Me110s were dive-bombing the place".

In the battle which followed each pilot bagged one Hun and the combat reports showed three Dornier 17s, two Junkers 88s, four Messerschmitt 109s destroyed. No losses to 32. It was time to celebrate.

A scene at Croydon after the raid on August 15, 1940. Children view a buried shelter which saved five lives. Notice the large holes in the side of the house. (Photograph: Imperial War Museum)

Time for a pint

August 15, 1940

AT nine o'clock on the evening of August 15, 1940 the BBC described the day's score in great detail. A few pilots heard the News in the bar of the Mess but the majority were crowding around the wireless in the White Hart at Brasted, a favourite haunt for Michael Crossley and the Station Commander, Group Captain Dick Grice. 32 Squadron, always there in force, were saddened by the absence of the CO's namesake, "Grubby" Grice but they knew this popular pilot enjoyed the occasional swim. It was the third time he had been shot down.

Pilots from 610 Squadron were also in the pub to talk about the versatility and deceptive toughness of the Spitfire and how this outstanding machine had helped to stop the German wave destined for the home airfield. They would have been outnumbered that night by supporters of the Hurricane. It was an interminable argument that continued long after closing time.

It is certain that talk in the White Hart that night would have included the Luftwaffe's mass attack on Tyneside where 79 Squadron was now stationed. The former "Bump" pilots had savaged a large formation of Heinkel 111's escorted by long range Me110's. So thoroughly did they complete the rout that 18 were destroyed without loss and the Luftwaffe never again attempted a daylight raid on the north-east.

While the boisterous young pilots were celebrating, there was plenty of activity at Biggin Hill. Engineers and ground crew in the hangars were busy patching up the injured Spitfires and Hurricanes. There were holes to plug with wax, hydraulics to fix and magic grease to be applied. The CO wanted two complete squadrons by dawn the next day so the men toiled all night snatching sleep in the hangar whenever they could.

The only thing to lure them away from their vital work was the approach of closing time and the close proximity of two pubs was always welcome. Many young fitters would slip through the hedge for a couple of pints at The Jail while others would stride purposefully down the road to the Black Horse. Then it was back to the unending struggle in the hangar.

The Jail Inn at Biggin Hill as it would have looked in 1940. The landlady was a great friend to the pilots, throughout the war. (Photograph: John Nelson)

The fields of Kent were littered with crashed aircraft but work on the farm must continue. This is the tailpiece of the Leaves Green Dornier which crashed on August 18, 1940, guarded by a soldier (see inset)

The men of the Home Guard, who, according to wartime propaganda, brought down the Dornier bomber at Leaves Green. The German pilot thought otherwise — see page 56. (Photograph: RAF Biggin Hill)

Gotya!

August 18, 1940

THE Luftwaffe promised Kenley that it would receive its package of bombs and, on Sunday morning August 18, it was as good as its word. Every man and woman at Biggin Hill knew it was their turn next, a feeling which became a reality when the Controller saw on his plot more than 50 Dorniers on course for the airfield.

"Jacko Squadron Scramble. Dogrose Squadron Scramble. Protect base."

Twelve Hurricanes of 32 Squadron and 15 Spitfires of 610 Squadron were airborne within minutes to intercept the enemy. Most of the ground crew, domestic staff, Waafs and storemen walked purposefully, but reluctantly, to the air raid shelters. The kitchen staff followed leaving the Sunday dinners in the oven.

The anti-aircraft unit of the 58th Heavy AA Regiment swung their guns towards the sky, holding fire initially because of the British fighters overhead. At the foot of Brasted Hill some six miles away, Geoffrey Durtnell, John Jenkins and their colleagues in the Observer Corps were already at their post. Eyes, experienced in spotting the unmistakeable sign of the Hun, stared into the clear skies. Outside the perimeter gate at Biggin Hill Lieutenant Bertie Miller of the 4th Platoon of the Kent Home Guard ordered his men to fill their aged rifles with ammunition and line the road.

The bombers appeared and stick after stick rained down on Biggin Hill. One Dornier 17 ventured particularly low. Gliding in over Leaves Green and already damaged by the ground defences from Kenley, it met a furious fusillade from Bertie Miller and his 19 men, some standing, some kneeling either side of Church Road.

After many weeks of intensive training the Home Guard were pleased to have a real target and pumped 180 rounds at the lame Dornier. Smoke came from the tail and the bomber burst into flames and rolled over as it crashed at Leaves Green. The Home Guard, cheering wildly, rushed to the Dornier and got there in time to see the pilot and crew pulled out and taken to sick quarters for treatment.

Bertie Miller, aged 90, and (right) the man he helped to shoot down! Herr Rudolf Lamberty.

Who shot down the Leaves Green Dornier?

DID Bertie Miller and his part-time soldiers really shoot down the Dornier bomber which rolled upside down as it crashed near Leaves Green? No book on the Battle of Britain, it appears, is complete without a mention of this romantic story. Certainly the Air Ministry, at the time, gave Bertie's men credit for the "kill" but that was part of the wartime propoganda.

The report in the Daily Telegraph of August 20, 1940 says the actual shooting was done by 20 out of 50 members of the Guard who were in trenches on either side of the crossroads. They included caddies from the nearby golf course, clerks, milkmen, two postmen and boys on holiday from Malvern College.

Bertie Miller himself has no doubt that his men administered the fatal shots. Still going strong at 90, he recalled the incident in great detail. "I gave the order to fire", he said, "and we pumped 180 rounds towards the belly of the bomber. When it came down and the crew stepped out alive, they looked rather arrogant. Certainly Harry Willoughby didn't like the look of the blond pilot".

Information gathered after the incident gives equal credit to Kenley ground defences and attacks from Sergeants Dymond and Brown of 111 Squadron. The most authentic story comes from the horse's mouth, the blond pilot, Herr Rudolf Lamberty who returned to Biggin Hill and explained how he was taking part in a two-wave attack.

"The first was due to come in and pound the airfield but due to a navigational error it failed to arrive. I was with the second wave, intending to sweep in at tree-top height and complete the job of demolishing Biggin Hill. I was attacked by a Spitfire and then met the full force of the defences from the ground".

The bomber with its fuselage flaming crashed at Leaves Green and Lamberty and his crew were taken to hospital. After treatment he was transferred to a POW camp in Canada. Photograph shows Lamberty with part of the bomber, presented to him at The White Hart, Brasted in September 1971. Above Bertie Miller in 1990.

Heroine with the Flags

THE raid on Biggin Hill on Sunday August 18 lasted barely ten minutes before it was finally repulsed by the Hurricanes and Spitfires of 32 and 610 Squadrons and the army gunners around the perimeter. The first bombs had fallen to the east, between the airfield and Downe, and had caused little damage. The second raid was more accurate. A Bofors anti-aircraft gun was hit, one of its crew killed and others wounded. The MT sheds were damaged and the airfield was littered with craters and unexploded bombs.

Sergeant (Joan) Elizabeth Mortimer was manning the switchboard in the Armoury and refused to move although she was surrounded by several tons of high explosive. The bombing became heavier but the WAAF Sergeant ignored the danger and continued to relay vital messages around the defence posts.

As the raiders departed but before the All Clear sounded Sergeant Mortimer walked and ran around the airfield with a bundle of red flags. Where a bomb had not exploded she placed a flag nearby. Biggin Hill was like a minefield and the aircraft, still airborne, needed to know where to land. A bomb exploded nearby, winding her and for a while she could not walk. When she recovered she continued planting flags. She was ordered to leave the area by an officer who said it was too dangerous. She carried on when he walked away.

For her courage and coolness Elizabeth Mortimer won the Military Medal, one of three to be awarded to WAAFs at Biggin Hill that summer. She had been at the station for almost a year arriving in September 1939 in rather unusual circumstances.

Miss Mortimer had previously worked in the Armoury at Hendon where 601 was based. She heard that the Squadron was to be posted to Biggin Hill and, with her friend Beryl Dobell, was determined to join them. Their colleagues in the Armoury thought there was little hope but the girls were determined to try.

Elizabeth and Beryl asked for a transfer but did not wait for the official confirmation. They drove through the night to the gates of Biggin Hill and when 601 Squadron arrived they calmly accompanied the boys into the station. The CO at Hendon considered them "lost" until she discovered their whereabouts six weeks later!

At Biggin Hill a surprised adjutant politely sent them to find a billet and told them to report back. Believing the adjutant had more important matters on his mind, such as the possibility of war, they stayed out of his way.

Elizabeth Mortimer, one of the first WAAFS at 'The Bump" was also the first to win the MM. Her citation read: This airwoman displayed exceptional courage and coolness which had a great moral effect on all those with whom she came into contact."

Elizabeth Mortimer — exceptional courage

Three pilots of 32 Squadron in their dispersal hut seem quite relaxed as they read or write .... but in August 1940 the atmosphere was electric! (Photograph: RAF Biggin Hill)

Humph the hero

August 18, 1940

THERE were plenty of heroes on the day that the Luftwaffe bombed Biggin Hill. The young pilots who were sent up to protect their base were outnumbered by five to one but in a "show" that lasted barely 10 minutes the two squadrons bagged at least nine Huns and sent many others fleeing back across the water.

In the air there was no greater feat than that of Flight Lieutenant Humphrey "Humph" Russell who had joined 32 Squadron at Biggin Hill in 1936 and was seconded to Control before the start of the war. Humph rejoined 32 on August 17 and the next day was experiencing his first operational sortie.

He destroyed an Me109 but during the combat a cannon shell exploded in his cockpit. Russell, seriously wounded in the leg, baled out and was taken to Edenbridge Hospital where the doctors were astounded by his ingenuity. Blood had been gushing from his wound but as he was floating to earth Humph Russell contrived a tourniquet to stop the bleeding. His Hurricane crashed at Skeynes Park Farm.

"Polly" Flinders, the man who had given the Polish pilots their first conversion course in a Hurricane and was in charge of the training flight, almost missed the action. Some time after the Spitfires and Hurricanes were airborne Flinders taxied out, caught up with a lone Dornier 17 and emptied most of his ammunition into it. He then chased another Hun over West Malling, Detling and Canterbury with the German pilot making frantic barrel rolls in an attempt to shake off the aged Hurricane. Flinders caught up and let fly with his remaining rounds. They were sufficient.

Meanwhile John Ellis of 610 was tackling the escorting Me109s at 31,000 feet before being ordered to join the party. There he chased a Heinkel 111 right across Kent before sending it into the sea.

In an evening scramble 32 Squadron Leader Michael Crossley was attacked by an Me109 and white smoke poured out of his exhaust signalling a glycol leak. Crossley baled out, watched his beloved Hurricane crash and was met by a hostile crowd in Gillingham who thought he was a Messerschmitt pilot. "Red Knight" Crossley was most grateful when the reception party put their pitchforks away!

On this day five pilots of 32 baled out and six valuable Hurricanes were lost.

On duty in the Salt Box gun post, Bill Brooker (left) and Reg Hume. (Photograph: Elizabeth Mortimer)

Flying Officer Douglas Grice "Grubby" had managed to bale out of his blazing Hurricane on August 15, 1940. Severely burned on his face and hands he landed in the sea and was kept afloat by his Mae West until an air-sea rescue launch picked him up and took him to the Royal Naval Hospital at Shotley.

This was Grubby's third big adventure. On June 6 return fire from a Heinkel badly damaged his Hurricane and he managed to glide 15 miles across France before landing in a small village. He met some soldiers who drove him to Rouen and then, with another officer, he travelled from aerodrome to aerodrome looking for an aircraft that would take him to England. At Dreux, after a journey of 400 miles, he found the HQ of the Allied Expeditionary Air Force. He was put on a DH Rapide returning to England but it diverted to Jersey to avoid black smoke from burning oil tanks at Le Havre. They flew on to Hendon two days later. He was awarded the DFC on June 25.

On July 4 Grubby was shot down again but this time he force-landed at Manston. After recovering from the injuries sustained on August 15 he returned to Biggin Hill as Controller.

When Sergeant Ronnie Hamlyn (above) crashed his Spitfire on landing at Biggin Hill in August 1940, he was charged with negligence and ordered to report to the CO. As he awaited his punishment (usually a fine of £5), Hamlyn heard over the tannoy: "610 Scramble". He excused himself, jumped into a Spitfire, entered straight into the attack and shot down two enemy aircraft.

Hamlyn reported to the CO when he landed but was again scrambled. This time he shot down one more 109. Reporting for the third time, Hamlyn was called into the office and stood there nervously while Group Captain Grice considered the charge. 610 was called for battle again and this time Hamlyn claimed two more destroyed.

Eventually the CO confronted his man, spoke to him sternly and told him he was being recommended for an immediate DFM! Hamlyn was commissioned in 1941 and went on to take command of the Air Sea Rescue Squadron, 276.

Au revoir 32

August 25, 1940

A memorable chapter in the history of RAF Biggin Hill closed on August 25, 1940 with this entry in the diary of the incomparable 32 Squadron.

'Well, old Biggin Hill, 32 (F) Squadron bids you farewell. You brought us honour, excitement, fear, depression, happiness, tragedy, laughs, new associations, thrills — in short, every sentiment a man can experience in quick jumbled succession. Do we regret leaving you? Do the happiness and elation you brought us outweigh the sorrow and pain and the indescribable "eat, drink and be merry for tomorrow we die" sensation that each day brought? We don't know. We think perhaps not.

No, we wouldn't have you again for worlds, but we wouldn't have missed you! You made men out of boys and we're grateful. So long, Biggin Hill. 32 Squadron will never forget you'.

And Biggin Hill will never forget the "32nd Pursuit". For nine incredible years it had been on "The Bump" and was to say farewell as the top-scoring squadron in Fighter Command with 102 enemy aircraft destroyed. Acting Squadron Leader Michael Crossley had the DSO and five others the DFC. Three pilots had been killed and one was a prisoner of war.

There was one last duty to perform before 32 left for the comparative peace of Acklington — a small matter of 12 Dornier 215s and 36 Me109s to intercept over Dover. As Crossley led his pilots on their final patrol from Biggin Hill thoughts inevitably turned to the farewell party later that evening in the White Hart.

One pilot did not attend the party. In fact he didn't get to Acklington. Pilot Officer Keith Gillman, a 20 year-old who had been with 32 Squadron since May 10, failed to return from the combat over the Channel.

Returning to Biggin Hill was 79 Squadron under the command of Squadron Leader John Heyworth. They left Acklington at dawn on August 27 and on the way south were diverted to Hawkinge. The next day they flew out to sea and destroyed two Heinkel 59s and two E-boats. Heyworth and his Hurricane pilots did not know they had a distinguished audience. High on Shakespeare Cliff with the Observer Corps were two men watching the "show" through binoculars — the mayor of Dover and the Prime Minister, Winston Churchill.

Welcome home 79 Squadron.

This photograph of Pilot Officer Keith Gillman was well-known during the war years as one that epitomised both the courage and the cheerfulness of the British fighter pilot. Gillman from Dover was 19 when he failed to return from combat over the Channel on August 25, 1940 — 32 Squadron's first pilot to be lost in the Battle of Britain.

The Daily Telegraph

and Morning Post

No. 26,592   LONDON, TUESDAY, AUGUST 27, 1940

BROADCASTING—Page Two   ONE PENNY

5 A.M.

LONDON'S LONGEST RAID WARNING

ENEMY RESORTS TO "NUISANCE" TACTICS

46 NAZIS SHOT DOWN YESTERDAY

ANOTHER BERLIN ALARM: EIRE VILLAGES BOMBED

London's longest air raid alarm of the war ended in the early hours of this morning. For more than six hours searchlights formed a wall of light round the Metropolis, seeking elusive Nazi 'planes which flew over at great height.

'Planes approached one or two at a time, taking turns to ring London, but very few bombs were dropped. It is thought by this form of night raiding the Nazis are now trying to exploit their "nuisance" value to hold up British production.

In the West End and Central London theatres and cinemas continued their programmes to the normal conclusion, while in the hotels and restaurants midnight cabarets and dancing went on without interruption.

The raid was the climax to a day of fierce air fighting in which three main mass attacks were made on Britain. The Air Ministry announced at 2.45 this morning that the day's bag totalled 46 enemy 'planes. Fifteen R.A.F. fighters were lost, but the pilots of 11 are safe.

Berlin also had an air-raid alarm, the second in two days. It lasted for 36 minutes and, according to the B.U.P. correspondent in the German capital, not a single anti-aircraft gun was heard and no 'planes were sighted.

Broadcasting from Berlin last night, the correspondent of the Columbia Broadcasting Corporation stated that three streets were roped off yesterday after Sunday night's raid. It was impossible, he added, to get near enough to see why.

Despite the neutrality of the Eire Government a single German raider yesterday bombed four villages in the neighbourhood of Wexford, wrecking a creamery and killing three girls. Dublin has lodged a protest in Berlin demanding "full reparation."

Invasion Threat Persists—Back Page. London Raid Damage and Battle off Portland—Page Three.

THEATRES CARRY ON

DAILY TELEGRAPH REPORTERS

For hour after hour during the night searchlights blazed brilli-   homes the moment the "all clear" sounded.

BOMBS exploding on the sea front at Folkestone during yesterday's raid, in which six houses were razed to the ground. Five German 'planes are believed to have been shot down.

9 HURRICANES FIGHT 150

DEFIANTS' BAG AT DOVER

Defiant fighters took part in yesterday's big air battles. They met nine Dornier 17 bombers as they approached Dover and shot down three and probably four.

Three waves of raiders were flung against South and South-East England yesterday. The first spread themselves along the Kent coast, flying inland over Canterbury, and were met by Spitfires.

The second big engagement of the day was fought partly over the Thames Estuary and partly inland over Essex and Sussex, a big force of raiders being prevented from reaching London. While this engagement was in progress London had an air raid warning.

The new Czech squadron, fighting its first engagement, shot down a Dornier and a ME 110 over East Anglia.

Nine Hurricanes made head-on attacks against 50 Dornier 17 bombers and 100 ME 110s flying over Essex. They attacked as a team, shooting down two bombers and crippling three more.

The Spitfire squadron, which on Sunday brought down 12 raiders in one fight, fought in the third battle, an afternoon attack on the Portsmouth area. It met 150 enemy bombers and fighters. Four Heinkel 111s fell into the sea and three more were seriously damaged.

BERLIN RAID IN BAD WEATHER

FIRST GERMAN BOMBS ON NEUTRAL IRELAND

FROM OUR OWN CORRESPONDENT

DUBLIN, Monday.

Bombs dropped at four points to-day in County Wexford, in south-east Ireland, 130 miles from the Ulster border, marked the first German raid on neutral Eire.

Three girls were killed and one injured. A protest and a claim for reparations are being made in Berlin.

It is not known whether the German pilot was making a deliberate attack or thought he was bombing Ulster or some other part of the British Isles.

Foynes, the Atlantic air base on which the Germans are thought to have had designs since the flights made by the British Airways flying-boat Clare, is 110 miles from Wexford.

The following official statement was issued last night:

"A bomber aircraft of German nationality flew over the area of Campile, Ballynitty, Bannow and Duncormick, Co. Wexford, between 2 and 3 o'clock this afternoon. Bombs were dropped at each of these points.

"The co-operative creamery at Campile was wrecked. Three girls

In consequence of the prolonged air raid alarm in the London area production of The Daily Telegraph, in common with all London newspapers, was retarded last night and several editions would therefore reach subscribers in many districts later than the usual hour.

AIR CHASE OFF DOVER

FOLKESTONE RAID SEQUEL

From L. MARSLAND GANDER,
Daily Telegraph Special Correspondent

DOVER, Monday.

A savage dog fight broke out over the town and cliffs this morning at unpleasantly close quarters following a tip-and-run raid on Folkestone.

I was standing on a sea-front slope when a Messerschmitt streaked over the bluff just above my head, a Spitfire snarling on its tail. The Spitfire's eight guns were blazing.

All around me hidden machine-guns on the ground opened up. I was momentarily in a cone of fire. Spent bullets pattered around.

Far out at sea a machine spun down helplessly into the sea; inland down went a second ablaze, bits breaking off in mid-air. A dull explosion in the distance told that it had blown up.

Now M.T.B.s left the harbour, leaving white trails of foam behind them, to pick up any survivors from the fallen machine.

In these seaside towns, only a few minutes' flight away from German soil, the need for the utmost efficiency in the warning system is constantly demonstrated. This morning I counted 34 little silver machines overhead, tiny specks in the sky at 13,000 to 15,000ft. These were probably the formations making for Folkestone, and they were well over the coast in what seemed no time at all.

DIVE BOMBERS

MR. KENNEDY'S ESCAPE

EXPLOSIONS 300 YARDS AWAY

DAILY TELEGRAPH REPORTER

Bombs fell 300 yards away from a house in the country in Berkshire, where Mr. Kennedy, the American Ambassador in London, was staying during the week-end.

Mr. Kennedy, who had been working with his secretaries late at night, went into the garden of the house about one a.m. on Sunday, and looked at the display of searchlights and at the flares that were being dropped by enemy aircraft. He saw one bomber caught in the searchlights and there was violent anti-aircraft fire.

The staff of the house went to

HOW R.A.F. SWEPT THROUGH BERLIN BARRAGE

SERIES OF HEAVY EXPLOSIONS

FROM OUR OWN CORRESPONDENT

NEW YORK, Monday.

The promptitude with which the R.A.F. made a 1,300-mile flight and attacked Berlin following the indiscriminate dropping of Nazi bombs over London has greatly cheered Americans.

Despatches, sent by American correspondents in Berlin and published in this morning's papers in the United States, hint that the British attack—or, rather, series of attacks lasting in all 2hr 46min—disturbed the German capital much more than the official statements admit. The official statements, incidentally, showed considerable confusion and were changed several times.

Joseph Grigg, of the United Press, reports that the British bombers attacked Berlin in two waves, roaring over Hitler's Chancellery and other Government buildings in the heart of the city, while anti-aircraft guns blazed furiously and heavy bomb explosions echoed through the streets.

The British raiders, he says, swept through the barrage that appeared to have brought every anti-aircraft gun in Berlin into action.

The guns along the Unter den Linden and at the top of the Ministries in the Wilhelmstrasse thundered, and "a series of heavy explosions attributed to high ex-   was not in the capital at the time of the raid.

One of the first official German statements issued claimed that the only bomb dropped was an incendiary one, which destroyed a summer-house in the North Berlin suburb of Rosenthall. It was also asserted that the raiders mainly confined their activities to dropping pamphlets.

Later, however, it was admitted that several incendiary bombs were dropped on the outskirts of the city. At times the streets in the centre of the city were illuminated by flashes of gunfire, and tracer bullets streaked across the sky.

"From the information available," writes the New York Daily News, "it would seem likely that the British bombers attacked the Spandau arms factory and artillery park, four miles to the north-

A Daily Telegraph photograph taken on Monday August 26, 1940 of bombs exploding near the sea front at Folkestone. Six houses were destroyed by the raiders who were intercepted by Spitfires of 610 Squadron. In this combat Pilot Officer Frank Webster came down in flames and was killed. Pilot Officer Peter Else baled out of his blazing aircraft but was hit by another burst which shattered his left forearm. In hospital this was amputated just above the elbow. Five German aircraft were shot down in this raid over Folkestone.

(Courtesy of The National Newspaper Library)

The deadliest stage

August 30, 1940

THE last two days of August, 1940 stretched Fighter Command, 11 Group and especially the Biggin Hill squadrons to the limit, for the Battle of Britain was entering its most crucial stage. Vast formations of Me 109s were followed by wave after wave of bombers. At one time on August 30 overhead raids were reported by 48 Observer posts and the fighting was unsurpassed in its fury.

At noon that day 300 bombers and fighters came across the Channel and began to fan out over Kent and head for the airfields that protected London. 79 and 610 had plenty of warning and planned a head-on attack — a deadly and highly skilled form of warfare that called for both nerve and reflex. Approaching the enemy, the Spitfire pilots pressed their buttons from 300 yards range leaving themselves one second to break away. The effect on the enemy formation was devastating. Ten pilots claimed victories including Pilot Officer Pegge, Pilot Officer Eric Aldous, Sergeant Horatio Chandler and Sergeant Beardsley.

Flying Officer Teddy Morris, a South African, flew towards the enemy but did not leave himself enough time to evade and bounced off the nose of a Heinkel 111. The impact destroyed both Hurricane and Heinkel but Morris had managed to bale out and landed at Dorking with a broken leg. In hospital the injured pilot wondered why the German had declined to break formation. Pilot Officer "Dimsy" Stones provided the answer: "The pilot", he said, "was already dead!".

Some of the raiders got through and dropped their bombs causing considerable damage in the villages of Biggin Hill and Keston. The majority fell wide of the airfield. Biggin Hill braced itself for a return visit by the Luftwaffe. It came at six o'clock that evening.

Villages are saved . . .

ONE young Pilot Officer of 79 Squadron, William Millington from South Australia crash-landed his Hurricane at Conghurst Farm, Hawkhurst and was wounded in the left thigh and badly burned. He could have baled out; in fact he forced the hood back and prepared to jump but below him was a group of small villages around Tenterden. With flames licking his cockpit, Millington glided into a field and got out just before the tanks exploded. The villages had been saved and the 23 year.old was awarded the DFC. Two months later, on October 30, Millington was killed while serving with 249 Squadron.

To save valuable time breakfast was often brought out to the ground crew as they serviced the aircraft. Here, the tailplane of a 79 Squadron Hurricane makes a useful kitchen table.
(Photograph: RAF Museum)

39 die in shelter

August 30, 1940

THE third bombing of Biggin Hill was carried out, not by a formation of 300, but by nine Junkers 88s which had followed the Ashford-Reigate railway at low level before swinging north to take "The Bump" by complete surprise. The damage they caused was appalling.

The cookhouse, workshops and the Naafi were destroyed. Airmen's barracks, the sergeants' mess, and the Waafery were made uninhabitable. One hangar was blown up, two aircraft destroyed and most of the station's transport was set on fire. Worst of all an air-raid shelter crammed with airmen received a direct hit and was reduced to a yawning crater full of rubble and mangled bodies. The death toll was more than 39.

In the airwomen's trench where steel-helmeted WAAFs were packed together, an explosion blew out the entrance and in another blast the concrete walls caved in. Those inside were buried under stones and earth. The girls were wearing steel helmets and they lay in a heap in the dark waiting to be dug out.

After the first bomb the electric lighting failed and the emergency battery set was used. This faded after the third bomb. Gas and water supplies were also cut off. Villagers in Biggin Hill who had seen the formation of Junkers approaching following the Westerham Road ran to the air field as the all clear sounded.

The entombed WAAFs, under tons of earth rubble, were brought out one by one, the rescuers tearing frantically at the earth with their hands. Most of them were safe but dazed, shocked and badly bruised. A few were more seriously injured and one was dead.

The dead girl was a nursing orderly from Tasmania, Corporal Lena Button, who received the full force of the explosion.

The women were taken to the sick quarters and, as night fell, work began on the crater that was the airmen's shelter. By the light of vehicle headlamps trained on the rubble the bodies were carried out one by one. Eventually a team of miners was brought in, the job was so large — but there was no hope for those inside.

Group Captain Grice handed his house over to the WAAF officers whose quarters had been demolished. He had a grim duty to perform — arranging a mass funeral and telegraphing the parents of those who had been killed. The funeral was fixed for the following Sunday.

These bombs were collected by Flight Sergeant Hunt who posthumously received the George Medal. He was killed in October 1940 while attempting to defuse a bomb fitted with one of the first anti-interference devices.

Morphia for the living

THE Medical Officer's report to the Station Commander concerning the raids on August 30 and 31, 1940 included the following passages.

'As the first bomb exploded the lighting failed. The emergency battery set was put on but that also failed after the third or fourth bomb. Emergency torches were procured and lack of lighting held up proceedings considerably. The dead were stored in a separate room and an orderly detailed to take particulars from their identity discs. The injured were seen on entrance by the MO, and an orderly was detailed to carry out the requisite treatment. In this way 22 casualties were treated in 45 minutes.

Word was then received that a shelter had been hit and help was required. An opening was found but it was plain that the majority of occupants had been killed. Those who were living and within reach, were given a dose or morphia, several having the injections into the face as this was the only part of them above the earth and concrete. Six living men were taken out but two died soon after. One of these had to have his wrist amputated to free him at all. The rescue squads worked hard and were relieved by ARP teams from Orpington and then by a team of Welsh miners, upon whose arrival a great acceleration was noticed immediately. By 0200 hours most of the bodies had been recovered'.

The report went on to mention Dr J.C. Colbeck of Downe and Drs Grant and Mansi of Orpington who worked for hours performing amputations in cramped conditions with enemy aircraft still overhead.

One of the most welcome sights at Biggin Hill during the Battle of Britain was the Salvation Army mobile canteen which always seemed to be in the right place at the right time. After the first bombing of Biggin Hill, "Sally Ally" was waiting for the airmen and women to emerge from the trenches. Coughing from the dust and smoke they queued for "wads" and half pint mugs of tea.
(Photograph: RAF Biggin Hill)

Far away from the battlefields of Biggin Hill, Spitfires of 72 Squadron were being given their pre-flight checks. The Squadron had been ordered to leave the comparative peace of Acklington in Northumberland and join the fray down south by exchanging places with the Spitfires of 610. The picture here shows 72 Squadron en route to Biggin Hill from "Ackers". Below them is the north-east coast. The pilots landed at "The Bump" in the afternoon on August 31 and were astounded by what they saw. Only one runway was in use and that was pockmarked with craters. "Jerry" had paid yet another visit at noon that day. In the evening they were airborne and immediately lost two Spitfires. Flight Lieutenant F.M. Smith baled out wounded and badly burned during combat over Dungeness at 6.35pm. Thirty five minutes later Flying Officer Edgar Wilcox crashed in Hungerford Field, Chickenden Farm, Staplehurst. He was killed.

(Photograph: Fox Photos)

Biggin Hill, Battle of Britain 'veterans' of 72 Squadron include Flying Officer R. Deacon Elliott in command of 'A' Flight standing left of the labrador. On the right of the dog is Pilot Officer Basil Douthwaite. Sergeant Henry Pocock who was shot down the day after he arrived at Biggin is astride the aircraft. Deacon Elliott was to return to Biggin Hill in 1962 as the first Commandant of the OASC. This picture was taken by Fox Photos in 1941.

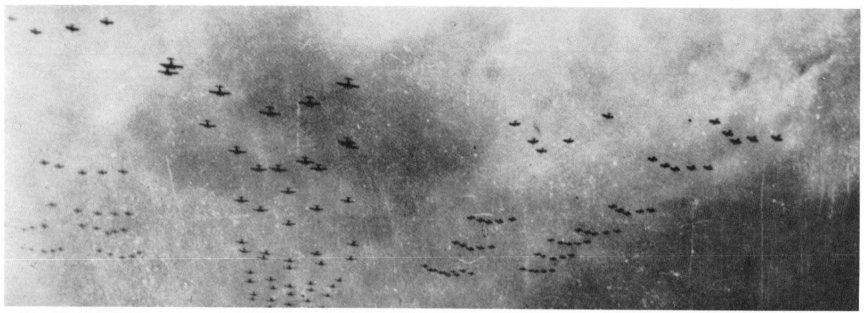

There are more than 100 German aircraft in this picture which was taken from Number Three Dispersal during the height of the raids on Biggin Hill. (Photograph: N. T. Freeman)

The living quarters after the raid of August 30 was part of the battlefield at Biggin Hill. New quarters were found for the airmen in huts on the South Camp which had been vacated by the Army. Three hundred more were billetted out in the villages of Biggin Hill and Downe. (Photograph: RAF Biggin Hill)

The 500 pounder

August 31, 1940

FOR some months "The Bump" pilots had monopolised all the glory. Now the heroes and heroines were becoming commonplace on the ground. Many of the WAAFs engulfed by tons of chalk and stone when their shelter collapsed were on duty next day. Among them was Corporal Elspeth Henderson who looked after the switchboard and the line to 11 Group headquarters. Another was Sergeant Helen Turner, a WRAF veteran of the 1914-18 war who manned the telephone in a small cubicle outside Operations Room.

There was Flight Lieutenant Osmond and his Signals Section who had worked all night to restore the vital links between Operations and H.Q, the Observer Corps and the radio transmitter and receiver. There were the WAAF cooks who had no gas, electricity or water and yet managed to provide hot meals for hundreds of people.

The runways were so badly cratered by the bombs that it was virtually impossible for the aircraft to land but while the Spitfires were "scrapping" many miles from home, every available man and woman set to work in-filling the craters. As they toiled they knew that the Luftwaffe had not yet finished with Biggin Hill. The systematic attacks, timed for mid-day, then six o'clock would continue.

They did. That evening controllers Roger Frankland and "Baron" Worrall plotted a small formation of ten Junkers 88s flying up sun. Within minutes the runways were cratered again, the station armoury was set on fire and four Spitfires destroyed.

In the Ops Room everyone was ordered to shelter. Sergeant Turner refused and remained at the switchboard. Another bomb fell outside and all lines except the direct one to Group HQ at Uxbridge were severed. Still Sergeant Turner sat at her post but not for long. She was dragged under a table protesting . . . as a 500lb bomb crashed through the roof and bounced off the safe. The blast knocked over Elspeth Henderson who was still in touch with Uxbridge. The plotting screen was smashed into tiny fragments, Ricocheting glass flew at Group Captain Grice and blood poured from his head.

The CO helped the WAAF Corporal to her feet, picked up his pipe and with the rest of Ops Room staff climbed out of a shattered window. There were fires everywhere. The station was devastated.

Sergeant Helen Turner was at her telephone switchboard just outside the Operations Room when a Warrant Officer dragged her under a table.

The station headquarters and the gable-ended hangar showing damage to the roof, caused, it is believed, by a motor car! On the morning of August 30, an officer carefully camouflaged his car and left it outside the hangar, by a tree, to dry. After the raid the tree had gone and the car was inside the hangar with its wheels in the air. The hangar was later completely destroyed. (See inset)
(Photograph: RAF Biggin Hill)

We'll blow up the hangar

September, 1940

THE funeral of the 39 people killed in the raid on August 30, 1940 was held at noon in the village cemetery at Biggin Hill on September 1. Friends and relatives had travelled many miles for the service, conducted by the Padre, the Rev Cecil King. The RAF was represented by Group Captain Grice and Assistant Section Officer Felicity Hanbury.

"Jerry", however, was far from finished with Biggin Hill and the wailing sirens soon sent the mourners scampering for cover. Four high explosives fell causing yet more damage but the coffins, draped with Union Jacks, remained undisturbed.

Before the All-Clear the Padre continued with the service. He ignored the sound of exploding bombs in the distance, the anti-aircraft fire, the noise of the battle overhead and the terrible thud as an aircraft hit the ground not so many miles away. He spoke calmly, without faltering, before the coffins were lowered into the ground.

The bombing of Biggin Hill continued day after day until there was nothing left to destroy except part of one hangar, the clothing equipment store and the remarkable resilience of Group Captain Grice and the 1,000 people who worked on "The Bump".

After the ninth or tenth raid and one more fatality, the CO came to the conclusion that the Luftwaffe would keep on coming until there was nothing but rubble below. At the same time Felicity Hanbury decided she should give the clothing away before the store was destroyed. Soon the clothing store was empty, and just in time. Twenty four hours later it was another smouldering heap. Now only the hangar remained.

Group Captain Grice made a drastic decision. He would blow up the hangar to save more loss of life. Explosives were put in place and at six o'clock on September 4 the CO ordered everyone to take cover. There was a giant explosion and the hangar collapsed. Biggin Hill was now totally flattened. The daylight raids virtually stopped.

The Air Ministry was not impressed with ASO Hanbury and certainly not with Group Captain Grice. An equipment officer claimed the clothing in the store had been removed illegally and the CO was censured at a Court of Enquiry for his unorthodox action.

The boys at the White Hart gave "Groupie" an enormous vote of confidence. Everyone agreed he deserved a bouquet — not a brickbat!

For courage and devotion

WHEN the station air-raid warning sounded on the morning of August 30, Felicity Hanbury, the Assistant Section Officer in charge of the WAAFS, was walking to her office half way between two trenches. She ran to one for cover and waited for the bombing to subside.

Even before the All-Clear the young WAAF officer clambered out to see how the airwomen were in the other trench. She smelt escaping gas and, to her horror, discovered it had been bombed and all the WAAFs blown to one end. One girl was dead and there were a number of serious casualties.

The airwoman's quarters had also been destroyed and ASO Hanbury had the immediate task of finding accommodation. She toured the village of Biggin Hill, knocking on doors and received tremendous co-operation. Billets were found for all. She comforted those whose lives were shattered by the experience but found that most of the girls were frightened only of showing they were frightened.

Soon after the bombing Felicity Hanbury was posted to London, survived the Blitz and later learned that she had been recommended for a Military MBE, the first such award to a WAAF Officer during the war, for "setting a magnificent example of courage and devotion to duty during the heavy bombing attacks experienced by the station". The citation continued: "The calm behaviour of the WAAFs during enemy action was outstanding and was largely due to the fine example set by this officer".

Felicity Hanbury was a young widow in 1940, her husband having been killed flying in 1939. She remained in the service after the war moving on to become Director of the WAAF from 1946-49 and Director of the reconstituted WRAF until her retirement in 1950 as Air Commandant Dame Felicity Hanbury. Later she married Sir Harold Peake, the late Chairman of the RAF Benevolent Fund. Today, Dame Felicity is the inspiration behind the formation of the Friends of the Imperial War Museum and her name is perpetuated at Biggin Hill as Hanbury Drive in the married quarters.

SUMMARY OF ENEMY AIR ATTACKS ON R.A.F. BIGGIN HILL

Date	Time	Number of enemy aircraft	Number & type of of bombs	Ground Defence in action	Summary of Damage
18 August, 1940	1330	30	500 (500 Kilo's max) including 90 D.A.	Yes	Direct hit on M.T. sheds. No other damage. 2 killed, 3 wounded. 90 D.A. bombs on aerodromes which remained operational.
22/23 August, 1940	03.25	1	H.E. Number not recorded	N/K	Bombs did not fall on A/D.
27/28 August, 1940	22.30	N/K	H.E. Number not recorded	N/K	None.
29/30 August, 1940	22.30	N/K	H.E. Number not recorded	N/K	Craters on A/D which remained operational.
30 August, 1940	12.25	N/K	H.E. Number not recorded	N/K	Surface of A/D damaged. Remained operational.
30 August, 1940	18.00	30	16 × 1000 lbs H.E. I.b. also dropped	N/K	Severe damage to workshops, equipment section, hangars M.T. sheds, barracks, dining halls etc. main and camp roads. Electricity, water, gas, sewage and telephone services severed. 3 air raid shelters hit, 39 killed, 36 wounded. A/D remained operational, temporary telephone and power hook-up arranged.
31 August, 1940	12.00	N/K	H.E. Numbers not recorded	N/K	Further damage to buildings and services. No casualties A/D operational.
31 August, 1940	18.38	204	H.E. Number not recorded	N/K	Further extensive damage to domestic and technical areas. Ops. room received direct hit, emergency Ops. room in Biggin Hill village brought into immediate use. 8 A/C destroyed on ground, seven personnel casualties. Telephone and power cables again severed. A/D remained operational.
1 September, 1940	13.00	N/K	4 H.E.	N/K	Damage to A/D surface, which remained operational further damage to buildings and temporary services.
1 September, 1940	18.00	N/K	H.E. & 1.B. Number not recorded	N/K	Further damage and casualties. Fires, but soon under control. A/D remained operational.
3 September, 1940	07.30	N/K	H.E.	N/K	Damage to roads. Practically no buildings left to damage. A/D remained operational, but all main services and communications destroyed.
3 September, 1940	10.30	N/K	H.E.	N/K	1 Killed. A/D operational. Main camp road cratered in 3 places.
5 September, 1940	10.03	40	H.E. & 1.B	Yes	Damage to dispersal points and A/D surfaces. Telephone lines destroyed. A/D operational.
18 September, 1940	08.03	1	12 H.E.	Yes	Slight damage to A/D which remained operational.
20/21 September, 1940	22.50	N/K	1.B.	N/K	No damage
6 October, 1940	12.45	1	8 H.E.	Yes	3 Barrack Blocks destroyed, slight damage to A/D surfaces.
12 October, 1940	16.30	1	5 H.E.	N/K	Very light. No details available.
16/17 October, 1940	19.30	N/K	H.E.	N/K	Camp road blocked
28/29 October, 1940	19.47	N/K	300 1.B	N/K	Nil
8/9 November 1940	18.53	N/K	4 H.E.	N/K	Very light. 1 Anson damaged.
10/11 November, 1940	22.10	1	16 H.E. & 1.B.	No.	3 aircraft destroyed, 10 damaged at dispersal.
7 January, 1941	15.40	N/K	9 H.E.	N/K	No damage
11/12 January, 1941	20.05	N/K	2 H.E.	N/K	No damage
19/20 April, 1941	21.45	N/K	1.B.	N/K	No damage
19/20 April, 1941	22.30	N/K	H.E.	N/K	1 D/A in centre of A/D. 1 Blenheim damaged.

TOTAL NUMBER OF AIR ATTACKS 25.

Many of the bombs at Biggin Hill had not exploded and they were carefully defused by a bomb disposal squad who discovered, to their astonishment, that some were British and dated from the early twenties. (Photograph: RAF Biggin Hill)

Luck ran out

September, 4

BY early September the Garden of England and the London suburbs were littered with the wreckage of enemy aircraft and many Nazi prisoners were held in town and village police stations. On occasions German airmen were taken to the Guard Room at Biggin Hill, having first been entertained in the Mess — a custom that continued throughout the war. Few of them, it seemed, appreciated the splendid Westerham Ale.

Unfortunately for the enemy, the driver of the 403 bus from Sevenoaks to Westerham was not quite so hospitable. Passing under a dog fight on the morning of September 4, he spotted a lone parachutist, his 'chute badly ripped, falling rather fast. By some miracle the Nazi landed on a haystack but that was his only piece of luck.

The driver stopped the bus and alerted the conductor. They armed themselves with spanners and approached the German who was struggling with his parachute and covered in hay. The man thought that London Transport uniform represented some kind of military organisation, gave a smart Nazi salute and announced that "Biggin Hill ist kapput". The bus driver, unfuriated by such cheek, hit him over the head with the spanner. The German airman recovered in the Guard Room at Biggin Hill.

On September 5, 1940, 72 Squadron flying from Croydon, lost Pilot Officer Winter who was killed attempting to abandon his Spitfire too low. It crashed at Elham in Kent.

Two Me109s were in collision during a combat south of Biggin Hill on Friday August 30, 1940. Both pilots baled out and were captured. The picture shows the remnants of the Messerschmitts at Layham's Farm, Biggin Hill. A few minutes earlier on the same day Pilot Officer Teddy Morris of 79 Squadron collided with a Heinkel 111. Morris baled out unhurt but his Hurricane was a write-off.

The Battle of Britain reached a new deadly phase on September 7. Infuriated by Bomber Command's surprise attack on Berlin, Hitler called off the offensive against the airfields and launched his air force against the heart of London. It was shortly after five o'clock that the Luftwaffe was heard above East London. More than 300 bombers and 600 fighters were following the Thames. They bombed Woolwich Arsenal, a power station, a gas works, the docks and the City. From the air London was a sea of flames. The Blitz had begun. (Photograph: Imperial War Museum)

A new Operations Room was set up in an empty shop in the village of Biggin Hill and the controllers and plotters carried on with chalk and a blackboard. But it was clearly only a temporary arrangement. Eventually the RAF, with some pressure from Lord Dowding, requisitioned a country house called Towerfields (above) at Keston Mark, some two miles from the airfield and converted it into a new Operations Block. After the war, broadcaster Richard Dimbleby, reporting from Towerfields, said: "This is the place from where you can truly say we won the war."

INTENSIVE CARE UNIT

OFFICERS' MESS
ROYAL AIR FORCE, BIGGIN HILL

Dated 2nd Sept. 19.40.   Account for August 1940.

Name F/O A.F. Jones

	£	s.	d.
Brought forward			
Messing	2	4	
Wines			4½
Tobacco, Minerals, Sundries		18	-
Library			
Telephone			
Mess Subscriptions		9	
Mess Contributions		10	½
Laundry		8	9
Newspapers			
Entertainments			
Billiards			
Sports Fund			
Silver Fund			
Garage			
Garage, Leaves Green			
Bridge Losses			
Batman			
Miscellaneous Bills			9
Benevolent Fund			9

RECEIVED WITH THANKS

Deduct Bridge Winnings

£ 4 16 5

Cheques to be made payable P.M.C., Officers' Mess, R.A.F., Biggin Hill, and crossed Lloyds Bank, Ltd., Bromley

Flying Officer Jones obviously enjoys his liquor! In August 1940 his salary would have been 11s. 10d. a day, equivalent to £4.14p weekly. There was a strict monthly limit of £5 on wine, hence the popularity of The Mess. It was known by some pilots as the 'Intensive Care Unit'.

An artist's impression of the Ops Room at Towerfields. (Photograph: RAF Biggin Hill)

High living — high flying

92 Squadron 8.9.40 to 25.9.41

Although he was only a Flight Lieutenant, Brian Kingcome found himself commanding officer of 92 Squadron on three different occasions. The first followed an incident when Squadron Leader Saunders tried to rub oil off the sleeve of his tunic by dipping a rag in 100-octane fuel. He then lit a cigarette, burst into flames and was taken to hospital. Kingcome became acting CO.
A few weeks later a new Squadron Leader arrived but on his second flight a bullet went through the floor of his cockpit, took the skin off his ankles, his knees and the tip of his nose. He went to hospital and Kingcome took over once more. Within three weeks the squadron had another leader but he was shot down on his third flight. Kingcome was CO again.
He is pictured above with Air Vice Marshal Sholto Douglas who was to take over from Dowding in November 1940 as head of Fighter Command. (Photograph: Imperial War Museum).

IF there was a change in Hitler's tactics, then there was also a change in Fighter Command's — certainly as far as Biggin Hill was concerned. 79 Squadron was posted away to Pembrey in South Wales for a rest and in its place came the "Ninety Second Foot and Mouth", full of panache and vigour, the squadron destined to become the most renowned in Fighter Command.

92 had been formed after the outbreak of war from the Auxiliary Air Force and Volunteer Reserve. It was commanded by Squadron Leader P.J. Sanders and then Squadron Leader A.M. McLachlan. Both ended up in hospital and Flying Officer Brian Kingcome took temporary control. Brian instilled into his squadron a tremendous spirit of gaiety. He was noted for his fighting and leadership qualities and he had that great gift of being able to make an order sound like a favour.

The Squadron was billetted in a large house nearby called Southwood where the pilots entertained the girls and even found their own squadron dance band made up of riggers, fitters and a few of their musical officers. On other occasions they would enjoy soirees in London's West End and, of course, they soon became loyal and enthusiastic customers at the White Hart in Brasted. Apart from Kingcome the regulars included Pilot Officers Bob Stanford Tuck, Tony Bartley, Bob Holland, a gifted pianist, and "Wimpy" Wade. They were usually accompanied by Zeke, Brian Kingcome's boozy bulldog who also liked a glass of beer.

After their pursuits of reconnaissance over the Bristol Channel and the Irish Sea, 92 Squadron pilots were delighted to be at "The Bump", but in the early days they flew alone for the station was too badly damaged to support two operational units. It was September 12 before 72 Squadron returned from its temporary posting at Croydon to form with 92 one of the most formidable partnerships of the Battle of Britain.

In the month of September alone 92 and 72 destroyed 60 enemy aircraft between them with 30 probables. The record number of kills in Fighter Command, then held by Michael Crossley's 32 Squadron, was eventually overtaken by the redoubtable fighters of 92 who, it appeared, only ever slept between scrambles — in their dispersal huts!

The Dornier 17 which force landed on the western slopes of the Darenth Valley above Shoreham just a few miles from Biggin Hill after combat with Spitfires on September 15, 1940. One German was killed and three captured. The badge below the cockpit is of the 8/KG76. Not far from the scene of this crash, at Lullingstone, there was a decoy airfield designed to fool the Germans. The Luftwaffe, however, knew of its existence.

Two of the Dornier crew which crashed at Castle Farm, Shoreham, Kent, Hans Pfeifer (left) and Martin Sauter were reunited at Treuchtlinger, Germany in 1984. Above: Another crew member is taken away by Stretcher. (Photograph: Jack Marriott)

They took their prisoner to The Crown

September 15, 1940

WHEN a message came through to the Otford First Aid Post that hop-pickers at Shoreham had been machine-gunned from the air, an ambulance left immediately to locate the incident. On the road to Castle Farm, the ambulance crew, Jack Marriott, Jim Edwards and Jack Boakes were diverted to a "new incident". A Dornier lay on the ground with a smashed undercarriage.

Three of the Dornier crew had been taken off by the Home Guard. The fourth lay beside the aircraft with bullet wounds in his chest. He was carried by stretcher (see picture) to the ambulance but he died on the way to Sevenoaks Hospital.

Colonel "Benny" Greenwood and his Home Guards were entrusted with one of the three uninjured German airmen. He was pale and very shaken so they stopped off at The Crown in Shoreham and bought him a brandy before turning him in!

Photograph above left shows Fw Hans Pfeifer and Fw Martin Sauter at a reunion in Treuchtlingen, Germany. They were two of the crew of that crashed Dornier and were meeting each other for the first time since their days in a POW camp. Photograph by courtesy of the Shoreham Air Historical Museum which has a full record of the incident.

September 15, 1940

**'One of our great days . . . .
the most brilliant and fruitful of any fought
upon a large scale by the fighters of the
Royal Air Force'**

– Winston S. Churchill

A look of grim satisfaction is written all over the face of Flight Lieutenant John Ellis as he inspects the remnants of the two Me109s which crashed at Biggin Hill after colliding in mid-air. On August 30 — the day that Hitler launched his deadliest attack on Biggin Hill — 610 Squadron, led by Ellis joined the Hurricanes of 79, shared 10 successes and chased many raiders back to the sea. Four days later on September 3, Ellis received the DFC from the King. In 1941 he went to the Middle East and served with the Desert Air Force until appointed to lead a Wing in Malta in 1943. He went missing in June of that year and was later reported to be a POW. (Photograph: RAF Biggin Hill)

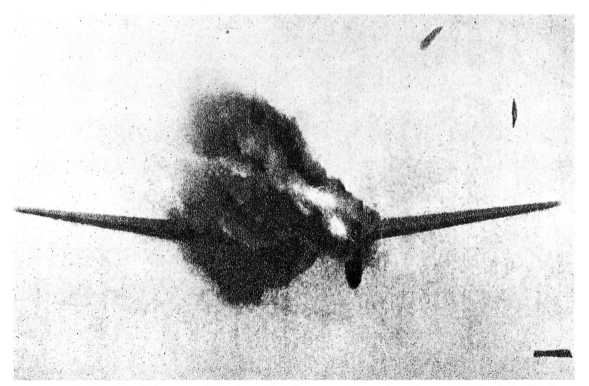

Among the German fighters and bombers shot down on September 15 were 15 Heinkel 111s. In the evening on the wireless the BBC said that "Jerry has got his come-uppance. The war is not yet lost".

81

The tide is turning

September 15, 1940

SUNDAY September 15, 1940, celebrated each year as Battle of Britain Day, was a climax to the aerial assault of Great Britain. One month earlier the Luftwaffe was confident of wresting air supremacy from the RAF but the violent nature of the battles of September 15, the Luftwaffe losses and the new-found confidence and combat power of Fighter Command suggested that this supremacy might not be gained at all.

The Prime Minister, with his genius for timing, chose this day to visit No 11 Group HQ and watched Air Vice Marshal Park and his staff direct the battle. It was just three weeks since Churchill's stirring speech to the House of Commons had immortalised "The Few" as changing the tide of war.

Now on this tense morning he watched the plotting table as more fighters were scrambled before noon than at any time in the battle. At Biggin Hill, 72 and 92 Squadrons were ordered to rendevous over base with Brian Kingcome "driving the train". They soon spotted a giant, compact formation of bombers with the fighters below.

In the battle that followed and others later that day the two squadrons shared a "bag of nine" confirmed destroyed and 12 damaged. Two Spitfires flown by Flight Sergeant Charles Sydney and Pilot Officer Tony Bartley were damaged but repairable. One was lost. Bob Holland of 92 baled out and was injured on landing and taken to hospital at East Grinstead.

Churchill watched every move of the battle on this historic day and in the evening learned that the score was 183 enemy shot down for the loss of under 40, a figure that was amended after the war to 56 — 26. Two days later Hitler issued the signal which postponed the invasion of Britain.

"The enemy air force is by no means defeated, on the contrary it shows increasing activity. The weather situation as a whole does not permit us to expect a period of calm. The Fuhrer has therefore decided to postpone "Operation Sealion" indefinitely".

The tide was turning.

It was on September 15 that a Dornier bomber, which was losing power after a raid on London, was attacked by six British fighters. Part of it fell in the forecourt of Victoria Station and the tail unit on to a rooftop in Vauxhall Bridge Road. It became the most famous German casualty of the war.

Sergeant Ralph Havercroft, better known as "Tich" and caught here without any trousers, was one of the great characters of Biggin Hill. Before he joined 92 Squadron he flew Blenheims but he was rather hampered by lack of height. He transferred to Spitfires and found that by sitting on his parachute he had a perfect view of the approaching Hun. (RAF Biggin Hill)

Defiants returned to Biggin Hill on September 15, 1940, as night-fighters. With them came 141, the original 'Cock' Squadron which was born at "The Bump" 22 years earlier. (Photograph: RAF Biggin Hill)

Sergeants George Laurence and Wilfred Chard of 141 Squadron who shot down a Junkers 88 over Maidstone on September 17, 1940. The two congratulate each other on their night's bag and are cheered by the ground crew. In the background is the once much-maligned Defiant, now a successful night-fighter. (Photograph: Imperial War Museum)

Night fighters

September 15, 1940

THE original Cock Squadron, 141, which had been virtually annihilated in July was thrown into the fray once more. Still equipped with Defiants the Squadron came down from Turnhouse with its "B" Flight, ready for night operations in the defence of London.

The slaughter in July had signalled the end of the Defiant as a day fighter, for it was a sitting duck for the Me109. 141 Squadron, however, never lost pride in the aircraft — and this time they had

good reason to celebrate their return to "The Bump".

Flying Officer John Waddingham and his gunner, Sergeant Alfred Cumbers destroyed a Heinkel and bagged a "probable" on September 16. The following night, Sergeants George Laurence and Wilfred Chard shot down a Junkers following a chase that was plotted on the School blackboard in Biggin Hill village with "Stuffy" Dowding as a guest observer.

The Chief of Fighter Command was a little dismayed with the archaic Operations Room set up and ordered the conversion of Towerfields to be completed "poste haste".

A few days later 141 Squadron moved to Gatwick to continue night patrols and Biggin Hill remained a day fighter base until the end of the war.

Lt. M.E. Jacobs, a Jewish officer, dived from the breakwater at Folkestone and swam 300 yards to rescue Messerschmitt pilot Uffz Dilthey of 4/JG2. The picture shows the Lieutenant barefooted and wearing a great coat as he followed the armed guard carrying the Nazi. A second man who also assisted in the rescue was Lieutenant Len Ebbington. (Photograph: Daily Telegraph)

Jew rescues Nazi

September 23, 1940

WHEN 72 Squadron was ordered up to intercept Dorniers and their escorts during a bombing mission early on Monday September 23, Sergeant Norman Glew and Flight Lieutenant Ian Cosby shared the destruction of a Me109 and watched with satisfaction as it ditched in the sea just off Folkestone pier at 10am. Imagine their surprise when they read in the Daily Telegraph the next day this report by H.A. Flower.

"The day opened here with a thrilling air battle which spread wide over my head above the cliffs, and in which I saw two swift and brilliant British victories. Waves of German bombers and fighters were streaming overhead, encouraged by the bright clear morning weather.

"British fighters were manoeuvring on the fringes of the enemy formations and above and below them when a Messerschmitt fighter zoomed down and flew some 200 feet above my head, obviously trying to escape to sea.

"A prolonged rattle of machine gun fire, a blast of cannon shell in return — but the Messerschmitt shook. Then a Spitfire as graceful as a swallow, dived to 300 feet, got on the Messerschmitt's starboard quarter and fired another short burst into him.

"I ran to the cliff edge to see the Messerschmitt slide into the sea off the Folkestone Harbour breakwater. The Spitfire saw him "safely" into the water and then flew off to rejoin the battle in the clouds.

"Lieutenant M.E. Jacobs, a Jewish officer on duty at Folkestone saw the Messerschmitt crash. He flung off his tunic, dived off the breakwater and swam some 300 yards to the rescue of the Nazi pilot. He towed the wounded man to a fishing boat.

Wing Commander Ian Cosby who lives at Biggin Hill, close to the airfield was, and still is, surprised by the events of that day. "I was credited with a share of that Messerschmitt", he said, "but I had no idea that the German pilot had been rescued. It was a good day for 72 Squadron. We drove swarms of German bombers helter skelter back across the Channel and shot down several 109s.

The vapour trails of British and German fighters twisting in combat high over the orchards of Kent in September 1940. The tip of a church spire and weathervane can be seen in the foreground. (Photograph: Kent Messenger)

The Battle Rages

September 27, 1940

For three weeks, wave after wave of Luftwaffe raiders dropped their bombs on London, killing more than 7,000 people and injuring 9,000. The bombs fell impartially on rich and poor alike. The King and Queen were in Buckingham Palace when a bomb fell in the garden. The British Museum and 10 Downing Street were damaged and radio listeners heard a bomb hit Broadcasting House during the News. On Friday September 27 came the last of the great daytime assaults on London by big bomber formations. Many never made it to the capital that day, for they were met head-on by the Spitfires of 92 and 72 Squadrons in a series of explosive battles over the orchards of Kent.

The two squadrons, both on dawn readiness, were in their dispersal huts for some time — sitting or sleeping on their camp beds, waiting for the telephone to ring. Just before nine o'clock the Controller spoke to the squadron leaders and within minutes the Spitfires were heading towards a formation of Dorniers and a protective swarm of 109s.

The battle which followed exploded over the town of Sevenoaks and people who had just arrived for work stood outside their shops and offices watching the trails of smoke form crooked patterns in the clear blue skies.

Acting Flight Lieutenant James Paterson should not have been flying. During his first week at Biggin Hill he was shot down and baled out with his clothes on fire. His face was badly burned but he insisted on flying again. At 9.30 on the morning of September 27 his Spitfire crashed at Sparepenny Lane, Farningham. This time Paterson could not escape from his blazing cockpit.

Ten minutes later, Pilot Officer Ernest Males, Flying Officer Paul Davies-Cooke and Sergeant John White were engaged with several 109s in a snarling dog fight over Sevenoaks. All three Spitfires were hit by machine gun fire. Males crashed at Stepney and Davies-Cooke at West Wickham. They both died. White was luckier. His header tank was damaged but he made a successful forced-landing.

In the same battle, Flight Sergeant Charles Sydney was killed when he crashed in flames at Kingston while Pilot Officer John Mansel-Lewis limped back to Biggin Hill with a section of his tailplane missing. The Luftwaffe did not have things all their own way. In the morning sunshine the Spitfires accounted for 10 of the enemy and wrecks of blazing aircraft were scattered all over the Kentish orchards.

Goering and his Luftwaffe had taken a "lot of stick" in the past few months and there was more to follow, this time by courtesy of the RAF Gang Show which visited Biggin Hill. The late Tony Hancock made his theatrical debut in a gang show and is seen here pictured second from the left. (RAF Biggin Hill)

Wimpy's revenge

September 27, 1940

PILOT Officer "Wimpy" Wade, caught by Dornier crossfire in the battle of September 27, was forced to crash-land on Lewes Racecourse and his Spitfire somersaulted on impact. Wade was trapped upside down in the cockpit but fortunately the aircraft didn't catch fire. The 20-year-old clambered out and made his way to Lewes police station where he persuaded an officer to drive him to Biggin Hill.

Wade was in action again that afternoon, looking for revenge. Just after 3pm he chased a Heinkel 111 to tree top height and saw it plough through a hedge near Lympne. Wade circled the spot and saw all the four crew haul themselves out of the wreckage. They looked up and waved. They too had survived a heavy landing.

"Saucepans for Spitfires". Pots and pans are unloaded at the Ministry of Aircraft Production reception depot, following Lord Beaverbrook's appeal to housewives. (Photograph: Imperial War Museum)

One of the most experienced and distinguished fighter pilots to arrive at Biggin Hill with 72 Squadron was Desmond Sheen, an Australian who was promoted to Flight Lieutenant on September 3, 1940. Two days later, while temporarily based at Croydon, he baled out over Hawkinge, wounded, and his Spitfire crashed at Bladbean. Sheen was one of the first pilots to make a kill — he destroyed a Heinkel 115 over the North Sea on October 21, 1939. In April 1941 Sheen commanded 72 Squadron and in November 1942 he commanded RAF Manston.

The fighter fund

SOON after Lord Beaverbrook became Minister of Aircraft Production, he appealed to all housewives to surrender their saucepans to help with the production of fighters. Thousands of saucepans and other aluminium utensils were immediately forthcoming.

In addition many communities launched their own "Fighter Fund". In Bromley, a few miles from Biggin Hill, a local benefactor offered £500 if the town could raise £4,500 in a couple of months. Donations poured in — and the £5,000 mark (the cost of a Spitfire) was passed with ease, the benefactor Mrs Wheeler-Bennett donating £1,000.

Almost every day another new Spitfire would be delivered to Biggin Hill to replace those lost and fresh pilots posted to fill the shoes of those killed in combat. Both the station's aircraft losses and Roll of Honour grew depressingly large.

Bad day for 92

October 10, 1940

WILLIAM Joyce, alias Lord Haw Haw, whose wireless reports every night from Germany sought to undermine confidence in the BBC and the British Press had this to say to his estimated audience of six million on the evening of October 10, 1940. "A single reconnaissance aircraft, returning from photographing the holocaust of London, was attacked today by six Spitfires. Its gallant crew showed great courage in destroying three. The aircraft crashed in France but the photographs have been saved".

For once it was true. Three Spitfires of 92 Squadron went down in flames in combat with a single Dornier over Tangmere. The Squadron had found the snooper without difficulty and Pilot Officer Desmond Williams and Flying Officer John Drummond were the first to attack Tragically they collided in mid-air, crashed near Brighton and both were killed. Sergeant Walter Ellis dived on the Dornier but return fire hit his glycol tank and he too went down in flames. He was unhurt.

"Wimpy" Wade, Bob Holland and Johnny Mansell-Lewis then attacked the bomber and silenced the rear gunner. It escaped into cloud.

Flight Lieutenant Ken Gillies catches up with much needed rest in his dispersal hut. Ken, who was with 66 Squadron throughout his flying life, was commander of "A" Flight when he flew from Gravesend on October 4, 1940 to intercept a formation of He—111s off the east coast. His Spitfire crashed in the sea and Ken's body was washed ashore 17 days later. (Photgraph: Dizzy Allen)

Johnny's heroes

October, 1940

Flight Lieutenant Johnny Kent was not a popular man with his pilots but he began to lead them in combat and some weeks later shot down the Squadron's 100th hun. He soon became "one of the boys".

Flight Lieutenant Johnny Kent was awarded the DFC on October 25, 1940 and the next day transferred to Biggin Hill as the CO of 92 Squadron, now adopted by the East India Fund. His arrival caused considerable distress among the party-loving pilots of 92 who had been without a commanding officer for several months. In a big show-down Kent told them:

'I have studied my officers' behaviour with concern and frankly I think it stinks. You are the most conceited and insubordinate lot I have ever had the misfortune to come up against.

Admittedly you have worked hard and got a damn good score in the air — in fact a better score than any squadron in Fighter Command — but your casualties have been appalling. These losses I attribute to the fact that your discipline is slack; you never by any chance get some sleep; you drink like fishes and you've got a damn sight too good an opinion of yourselves.

My second-in-command puts up the biggest black I have ever experienced in my air force career, and none of you have the decency to inform me. When one of my flight commanders comes out of hospital, hobbles down to dispersal, throws down his crutches, uses his authority to demand an aircraft and takes off on a mission, I have no further use for him in my squadron.

On his own admission he was feeling weak and giddy, and his only excuse was that he wanted to prove to himself that he had not lost his nerve.

Now, your billets. It appears that you have turned the living quarters, which were allotted to you to provide a certain amount of security and rest, into a night club. It also appears that you ask your various lady friends down to spend weekends with you whenever you please. This will cease. All women will be out of the house by 2300 hours sharp.

Your clothes — I can scarcely call them uniform. I will not tolerate check shirts, old school ties, or suede shoes. While you are on duty you will wear the regulation dress. Neither will I tolerate pink pyjamas under your tunics.

You all seem to possess high powered automobiles. None of these appear to be taxed or insured, but I hear from the Adjutant that you have an understanding with the local police. Well, that may be, but how do you explain where you get your petrol from? Your cars reek of 100-octane, and I can assure you you're not fooling the Station Commander.

Finally I want to see an all-round improvement. At the moment I think you're a lot of skunks'.

Historians have decreed that the Battle of Britain began on Wednesday July 10 and ended on Thursday October 31, 1940. During those 113 days of constant action 45 pilots flying from the RAF base at Biggin Hill were killed and 46 wounded. 104 Spitfires and 51 Hurricanes were lost or damaged. Six Defiants were lost in the battle of July 19. Here is a day-by-day assessment of the losses.

Wednesday July 10: 610 Squadron Spitfire L1000 damaged. Squadron Leader A.T. Smith unhurt.

Friday July 12: 610 Squadron Sergeant S. Ireland killed. Lost control during dogfight practice and crashed in Titsey Park. Spitfire P9502 a write-off.

Saturday July 13: 610 Squadron Sergeant P.I. Watson-Parker killed during routine patrol. Spitfire R6807 a write-off.

Wednesday July 17: 32 Squadron Hurricane N2588 damaged. Flying Officer J.B.W. Humpherson unhurt.

Thursday July 18: 610 Squadron Pilot Officer P. Litchfield missing in combat over Channel north of Calais. Spitfire P9452 lost.

Friday July 19: 32 Squadron Sergeant G. Turner baled out badly burned. Hurricane P3144 a write-off.

141 Squadron, West Malling Flight Lieutenant I.D. Donald and Pilot Officer A.C. Hamilton killed. Shot down and crashed at Elmsvale Road, Dover. Defiant L7009 a write-off. Pilot Officer J.R. Kemp and Sergeant R. Crombie missing following combat off Dover. Defiant L6974 lost. Pilot Officer R.A. Hawley and Sergeant A.G. Curley missing following combat off Dover. Defiant L6995 lost. Pilot Officer R. Kidson and Sergeant F.P.J. Atkins killed during combat off Dover. Defiant L7015 lost. Pilot Officer J.R. Gardner baled out wounded and rescued from sea. Pilot Officer D.M. Slatter missing following combat off Dover. Defiant L7016 lost. Pilot Officer I.N. McDougall unhurt, Sergeant J.F. Wise missing following combat off Dover. Defiant L6983 damaged. Flight Lieutenant M.J. Loudon wounded, Pilot Officer E. Farnes baled out and rescued from sea. Defiant L7001 a write-off.

Saturday July 20: 32 Squadron Sergeant W.B. Higgins injured in action over Dover. Hurricane P3679 damaged. Sub-Lieutenant G.G.R. Bulmer missing after being shot down off Dover, Hurricane N2670 lost. Squadron Leader J. Worrall force-landed near Hawkinge, unhurt,

Hurricane N2532 a write-off. **610 Squadron:** Pilot Officer G. Keighley baled out and wounded in combat over Hawkinge. Spitfire N3201 a write-off.

Thursday July 25: 32 Squadron Pilot Officer V.G. Daw slightly injured. Forced-landed near Dover. Hurricane P3677 damaged. **610 Squadron** Squadron Leader A.T. Smith killed. Crashed on landing at Hawkinge. Spitfire R6693 a write-off. Pilot Officer F.T. Gardiner wounded during combat over Channel. Spitfire R6595 damaged.

Monday July 29: 610 Squadron Pilot Officer S.C. Norris unhurt. Spitfire P9503 damaged.

Tuesday August 6: 32 Squadron Hurricane V7205 force-landed at base, pilot believed unhurt, aircraft a write-off.

Sunday August 11: 610 Squadron Spitfire R6918 failed to return from Channel patrol, Flight Sergeant J.H. Tanner killed. Spitfire R6630 missing following Channel patrol, Sergeant W.J. Neville missing.

Monday August 12: 32 Squadron Hurricane N2596 shot down and crashed near Hawkinge, Pilot Officer A.R.H. Barton unhurt. **610 Squadron** Pilot Officer E.B.B. Smith rescued from sea, Spitfire L1044 lost. Spitfire R6806 damaged, Flying Officer F.T. Gardiner wounded. Spitfire R6621 damaged, pilot unhurt. Spitfire P9495 a write-off, pilot believed unhurt.

Wednesday August 14: 32 Squadron Hurricane P3171 severely damaged, Pilot Officer Smythe unhurt. Hurricane P3146 force-landed Hawkinge, Pilot Officer A.R.H. Barton unhurt. **610 Squadron** Spitfire K9947 force-landed at Wye, Sergeant B.E.D. Gardner wounded. Spitfire L1009 severely damaged, pilot believed unhurt.

Thursday August 15: 32 Squadron Hurricane N2459 shot down over sea, Pilot Officer D.H. Grice baled out, burned. Hurricane N2671 forced-landed, Pilot Officer B. Wlasnowalski unhurt. Hurricane P3522 damaged, Sergeant B. Henson unhurt.

Friday August 16: 610 Squadron Spitfire R6802 failed to return from combat off Dungeness, Flight Lieutenant W.H.C. Warner missing. Spitfire damaged, Pilot Officer D. McT. Gray unhurt.

Sunday August 18: 32 Squadron Hurricane P3147 set alight during action over Biggin Hill, abandoned over Brenchley, Pilot Officer J.F. Pain slightly wounded. Cannon shell exploded in cockpit of Hurricane V7363 in combat over Biggin Hill, Flight Lieutenant H.a'B. Russell baled out seriously wounded. Hurricane V6536 damaged in combat over Biggin Hill, force-landed at Otford,

Sergeant B. Henson slightly wounded. Hurricane N2461 shot down, Squadron Leader M.N. Crossley baled out unhurt landing at Gillingham. Hurricane V6535 shot down, Pilot Officer R.C.C. de Grunne baled out, badly burned. Hurricane R4106 crashed following combat over Canterbury, Sergeant L.H.B. Pearce wounded. Hurricane R4081 force-landed at base following combat, Pilot Officer A.F. Eckford unhurt. **610 Squadron** Pilot Officer C.O.J. Pegge unhurt when Spitfire R6694 hit and further damaged on landing. Spitfire R6993 damaged by cross-fire over Dungeness, Flight Lieutenant J. Ellis unhurt.

Thursday August 22: 32 Squadron Hurricane P3205 crashed on landing at Hawkinge, Pilot Officer J. Pfeiffer unhurt. **610 Squadron** Spitfire R6695 shot down during combat over Folkestone, Sergeant D.F. Corfe unhurt.

Friday August 23: 32 Squadron Pilot Officer J. Pfeiffer unhurt when Hurricane P2795 crash landed on one wheel at Hawkinge due to combat damage. Hurricane P3900 force-landed at Hawkinge, pilot unhurt.

Saturday August 24: 32 Squadron Hurricane shot down in combat, Pilot Officer K. Pniak slightly injured. Hurricane V6568 crashed at Lyminge, Pilot Officer R.F. Smythe wounded. Hurricane V6572 shot down, crashed at Rhodes Minnis near Lyminge, Pilot Officer K. Pniak baled out, injured. Hurricane V6567 crashed at Tedders Lees near Elham following combat, Pilot Officer E.G.A. Seghers baled out unhurt, landing in the sea. Hurricane P3481 crashed near Lyminge during combat over Folkestone, Squadron Leader M.N. Crossley unhurt. **610 Squadron** Spitfire R6686 crashed at Hammill near Eastry following combat off Ramsgate, Sergeant S.J. Arnfield baled out, injured. Spitfire R6641 returned to base damaged after combat off Dover, Pilot Officer E.S. Aldous unhurt. Spitfire X4102 shot down in combat over Dover and crash-landed near Shepherdswell, Pilot Officer D. McI. Gray wounded. Spitfire shot down in combat over Thames Estuary, Pilot Officer C. Merrick slightly wounded.

Sunday August 25: 32 Squadron Hurricane V6547 shot down in combat over Channel, Pilot Officer J. Rose rescued from sea. Hurricane N2433 failed to return from combat over the Channel, Pilot Officer K.R. Gillman missing. **610 Squadron** Spitfire K9931 shot down in combat over Dover, Pilot Officer F.T. Gardiner slightly wounded.

Monday August 26: 610 Squadron Spitfire R6595 crashed on attempting to land at Hawkinge following severe damage in combat over Folkestone, Pilot Officer F.K. Webster killed. Spitfire P9496 shot down in combat over Folkestone, crashed at Paddlesworth, pilot believed unhurt. Spitfire R6970 shot down in action over Folkestone and crashed at Castle Hill, Hawkinge, Sergeant P. Else seriously wounded.

Wednesday August 28: 79 Squadron Hurricane P3938 force-landed near Tenterden after combat over Hythe, Flight Lieutenant G.D.L. Haysom unhurt. **610 Squadron** Spitfire P9511 shot down in combat over Dover and crashed into a house at Stelling Minnis, Pilot Officer K.H. Cox killed.

Thursday August 29: 610 Squadron Spitfire X4011 damaged in combat, crashed at Gatwick, Pilot Officer A.C. Baker unhurt. Spitfire R6629 shot down and crashed at Hurst Green, Sergeant E. Manton killed.

Friday August 30: 32 Squadron Hurricane N2540 destroyed in enemy attack on base, no personnel losses. **79 Squadron** Hurricane P3203 crashed after combat over Reigate, Pilot Officer E.J. Morris baled out unhurt. Hurricane returned to base damaged following combat over Surrey, Pilot Officer W.H. Millington unhurt. Hurricane damaged during combat over base, Pilot Officer P.F. Mayhew unhurt. Hurricane V6624 shot down in attack and crashed at Smarden, Pilot Officer J.E. Marshall baled out unhurt.

Saturday August 31: 72 Squadron Spitfire P9438 crashed during combat over Dungeness, Flight Lieutenant F.M. Smith baled out wounded and badly burned. Spitfire P9457 shot down in combat over Dungeness, crashed at Staplehurst, Flying Officer E.J. Wilcox killed. **79 Squadron** Hurricane N2345 crashed at Limpsfield following combat over base, Pilot Officer G.H. Nelson-Edwards slightly injured. Hurricane V7200 shot down in combat over Kenley, Sergeant H.A. Bolton killed. Hurricane B3050 crash-landed after combat over Romney, Pilot Officer W.H. Millington wounded and badly burned. Hurricane P3877 damaged during attack over base and crashed on landing, Pilot Officer E.J. Morris wounded. Hurricane P3166 shot down during attack over Tunbridge Wells, crashed at Bedgebury Park, Squadron Leader P.W. Townsend baled out, wounded. Hurricane V6581 crashed between Northiam and Newenden after combat over Tunbridge Wells, Pilot Officer P.A. Worrall slightly wounded. Hurricane N2544 shot down in action over

Thames Estuary, crash-landed in flames, Pilot Officer W.T. Hodgson unhurt. Hurricane damaged in combat over Thames Estuary, Pilot Officer J.E. Marshall unhurt. Hurricane L2071 returned to base with fabric stripped from wings following vertical dive in pursuit of Bf110 west of Sittingbourne, Sergeant G.B. Booth unhurt.

Sunday September 1: 79 Squadron Hurricane crashed on landing following combat over base, Flight Lieutenant G.D.L. Haysom believed unhurt. Hurricane severely damaged in combat over base, Pilot Officer L.T. Bryant-Fenn wounded. Hurricane L2062 crashed following combat over base, Pilot Officer B.R. Noble wounded.

Wednesday September 4: 79 Squadron Hurricane P3676 severely damaged in action over base, Sergeant J. Wright wounded.

Thursday September 5: 79 Squadron Hurricane P5207 damaged in attack over base, Flight Lieutenant G.D.L. Haysom unhurt. Hurricane damaged in combat, Flight Lieutenant H.S. Giddings unhurt. Hurricane 314 damaged during combat over Kent coast, Flying Officer B.H. Bowring unhurt. Hurricane 312 force-landed near Lullingstone Castle following combat over north Kent, Sergeant F.H. Silk slightly wounded.

Saturday September 7: 79 Squadron Hurricane damaged, Pilot Officer D.W.A. Stones wounded.

Monday September 9: 92 Squadron Spitfire L1077 crash-landed near Rye following combat over base, Pilot Officer C.H. Saunders wounded. Spitfire P9372 shot down in combat over base, Pilot Officer W.C. Watling baled out badly burned. Spitfire R6596 severely damaged following combat over base, Pilot Officer B. Wright unhurt.

Wednesday September 11: 92 Squadron Spitfire K9793 presumed crashed into sea following combat over Dungeness, Pilot Officer F.N. Hargreaves missing. Spitfire R6613 crashed following combat over Folkestone, Flight Lieutenant J.A. Paterson believed unhurt. Spitfire P9464 shot down in combat and crashed at Smeeth, Pilot Officer H.D. Edwards killed.

Saturday September 14: 72 Squadron Spitfire K9960 crashed following combat over Ashford, Sergeant H.J. Bell-Walker baled out unhurt. **92 Squadron** Spitfire R6624 shot down and crashed near Faversham, Sergeant H.W. McGowan baled out wounded. Spitfire X4051 returned to base with damage after combat over Canterbury, Sergeant J. Mann injured.

Sunday September 15: 92 Squadron Spitfire R6767 damaged following combat over Canter-bury, Flight Sergeant C. Sydney unhurt. Spitfire P9513 damaged over Ashford, Pilot Officer A.C. Bartley unhurt. Spitfire R6606 shot down in combat west of Ashford, Pilot Officer R.H. Holland baled out, slightly injured.

Monday September 16: 92 Squadron Spitfire R6616 damaged on landing, Pilot Officer H.P. Hill unhurt.

Wednesday September 18: 72 Squadron Spitfire R6704 shot down in surprise attack during patrol over Gravesend, Sergeant H.J. Bell-Walker seriously wounded. Spitfire P9368 damaged in combat and force-landed at Dover, Pilot Officer J.P. Lloyd seriously wounded. Spitfire X4337 'bounced' over north Kent and force-landed at Hawkinge, pilot unhurt. **92 Squadron** Spitfire N3193 crashed and burned out at Hollingbourne following combat, Pilot Officer R. Mottram slightly burned. Spitfire N3283 severely damaged in combat and crashed at Appledore due to engine failure during forced-landing, Pilot Officer A.C. Bartley unhurt. Spitfire K9991 crash-landed at Debden following combat off Essex coast, Flight Lieutenant J.A. Paterson unhurt.

Friday September 20: 72 Squadron Spitfire X4410 shot down in combat over Canterbury, Pilot Officer D.F. Holland baled out and died shortly after admission to hospital. **92 Squadron** Spitfire X4417 shot down in combat over Dungeness, Pilot Officer H.P. Hill killed. Spitfire N3248 shot down into Channel off Dungeness, Sergeant P.R. Eyles missing.

Saturday September 21: 92 Squadron Spitfire N3032 believed force-landed near Hildenborough following combat over Sevenoaks, pilot unhurt.

Monday September 23: 72 Squadron Spitfire X4063 believed crash-landed and burned out near Sittingbourne following combat over Gravesend, Pilot Officer B.W. Brown unhurt. **92 Squadron** Spitfire P9371 crashed attempting forced-landing near West Malling following combat over Gravesend, Pilot Officer A.J.S. Pattinson severely wounded.

Tuesday September 24: 72 Squadron Spitfire severely damaged in combat over Swanley, Flight Sergeant Steere unhurt. **92 Squadron** Spitfire X4037 shot down crashed and burned out near North Weald, Pilot Officer J.S. Bryson killed. Spitfire X4356 damaged in combat over Maidstone, crash-landed on Higham Marshes, Sergeant W.T. Ellis unhurt, Spitfire X4427 severely damaged in combat over Maidstone, Squadron Leader R.C.F. Lister, returned to base wounded.

Friday September 27: 72 Squadron Spitfire X4340 shot down in combat over Sevenoaks, crashed at Stepney, Pilot Officer E.E. Males killed. Spitfire N3068 shot down during combat over Sevenoaks, crashed at West Wickham, Flying Officer P.J. Davies-Cook killed. Spitfire forced-landed following combat over Sevenoaks, Sergeant J. White unhurt. 92 Squadron Spitfire X4422 shot down in combat over Sevenoaks, crashed at Farningham, Flight Lieutenant J.A. Paterson killed. Spitfire X4480 damaged in combat over Sevenoaks, returned to base minus section of tailplane, Pilot Officer J. Mansel-Lewis unhurt. Spitfire P9544 force-landed at Lewes Race Course, Pilot Officer T.S. Wade unhurt. Spitfire R6767 reputedly crashed at Kingston-on-Thames following combat, Flight Sergeant C. Sydney killed. Spitfire R6622 shot down and crashed at Dartford, Sergeant T.G. Oldfield killed. Spitfire R6760 crashed on landing at base following combat, Sergeant H. Bowen-Morris unhurt.

Monday September 30: 92 Squadron Spitfire X4069 damaged in combat over Brighton, forced-landed at Shoreham, Pilot Officer B. Wright slightly wounded.

Saturday October 5: 72 Squadron Spitfire X4544 mid-air collision, Sergeant R.C.J. Staples unhurt. Spitfire K9989 mid-air collision Pilot Officer N. Sutton killed. Spitfire K9935 damaged over Channel, Flight Sergeant J. Steere unhurt.

Sunday October 6: 72 Squadron Spitfire K9940 severely damaged in bombing attack on base, no personnel casualties.

Tuesday October 8: 72 Squadron Spitfire K9847 force-landed at Halstead, Sergeant N.V. Glew unhurt. Two Spitfires damaged in combat, pilots unhurt.

Wednesday October 9: 92 Squadron Spitfire shot down at Ashford, Sergeant E.T.G. Frith baled out badly burned.

Thursday October 10: 92 Squadron Spitfire X4038 involved in mid-air collision, crashed east of Brighton, Pilot Officer D.G. Williams killed.

Friday October 11: 72 Squadron Spitfire K9870 shot down during combat off Deal, Pilot Officer H.D. Pool wounded. Spitfire R6777 taxi-ing accident prior to take-off, Sergeant N.V. Glew unhurt.

Saturday October 12: 72 Squadron Spitfire P9338 crashed near Folkestone, Pilot Officer H.R. Case killed *92 Squadron* Spitfire X4591 shot down in combat over Hawkinge, Pilot Officer A.J.S. Pattinson killed.

Tuesday October 15: 92 Squadron Spitfire R6642 shot down in combat over Thames Estuary, Sergeant K.B. Parker killed. Spitfire R6838 shot down in combat, Flight Lieutenant C.B.F. Kingcome baled out wounded. Spitfire shot down off Allhallows, Pilot Officer J.W. Lund rescued from sea.

Thursday October 17: 74 Squadron Spitfire II P7360 shot down over Maidstone, Flying Officer A.L. Ricalton killed.

Saturday October 19: 92 Squadron Spitfire R6922 crashed at Smarden, Sergeant L.C. Allton killed.

Sunday October 20: 74 Squadron Spitfire II P7370 shot down in combat over Maidstone, Sergeant T.B. Kirk baled out severely wounded later died. Spitfire II P7426 shot down over south London, Sergeant C.G. Hilken baled out wounded. Spitfire II P7355 severely damaged during combat over south London, Pilot Officer B.V. Draper unhurt. **92 Squadron** Spitfire N3113 shot down at Horsmonden, force-landed near Tonbridge, Flying Officer J.W. Villa unhurt. Spitfire X4412 shot down at Horsmonden, returned to base, pilot unhurt.

Tuesday October 22: 74 Squadron Spitfire II P7431 shot down and crashed at South Nutfield, Flying Officer P.C.B. St John killed. Spitfire II P7364 crashed at Hadlow Place near Tonbridge following combat, Pilot Officer R.L. Spurdle baled out unhurt.

Friday October 25: 92 Squadron Spitfire X4480 force-landed at Penshurst following combat, Pilot Officer J. Mansell–Lewis unhurt.

Sunday October 27: 74 Squadron Spitfire II P7368 force-landed after combat over Maidstone, Squadron Leader A.G. Malan unhurt. Spitfire II P7526 shot down in combat over Maidstone, Sergeant J.A. Scott killed. Spitfire II P7353 damaged during combat over Maidstone, Flying Officer W.H. Nelson unhurt. **92 Squadron** Spitfire R6721 force-landed near Effingham, Sergeant D.E. Kingaby unhurt.

Tuesday October 29: 74 Squadron Spitfire II P7385 force-landed, Sergeant H.J. Soars unhurt. **92 Squadron** two Spitfires collided in taxi-ing accident, Sergeants H. Bowen-Morris and D.E. Kingaby unhurt.

The supreme sacrifice – page 158

End of the battle

October 30, 1940

IF mid-October was a depressing time for 92 Squadron, then it was even worse for 72 which was reduced to seven pilots of experience. Since Males and Davies-Cooke had been killed in combat over Sevenoaks, the Roll of Honour now included Pilot Officer Norman Sutton who died in a mid-air collision with Sergeant Robert Staples and Pilot Officer Herbert Case, killed near Folkestone.

It was time for a rest and on October 13, 72 Squadron was ordered to Leconfield for operational training duties. In its place came the Tiger Squadron, No 74, led by Squadron Leader Adolf Gysbert Malan DFC and Bar, known throughout Fighter Command as "Sailor".

Born in South Africa, Malan went to sea at 15 with the Union Castle line, first as a cadet and then an officer. He joined the Royal Air Force in 1936, quickly qualified as a pilot and was nominated to collect the first production Spitfire from Vickers Supermarine. When he arrived at Biggin Hill he was considered to be one of the outstanding fighter pilots of the war and was approaching 20 kills.

His flight commanders were Flying Officer John Mungo Park — a 22-year-old Liverpudlian and Pilot Officer Harbourne Stephen, a Scot. Malan boasted that he had the toughest bunch in Fighter Command.

The Tigers (code name Dysoe) were more disciplined than the party-going socialites in the other squadron but they shared a common aim in combat and formed another formidable partnership.

Although October 30 was officially designated as the end of the Battle of Britain, the intensive bombing of British towns and cities continued without respite. Already more than 13,000 citizens had been killed and more than 20,000 injured. The pattern of fighting also continued until the Luftwaffe conserved its bombers for the night-time Blitz.

Britain remained unconquered and so did her most bombed fighter station, Biggin Hill. Group Captain Grice, taking a line from the Windmill Theatre, whose stars were frequent visitors to "The Bump," was proud to say:

"We never closed".

Sailor Malan, who commanded 74 "Tiger" Squadron, arrived at Biggin Hill on October 13, 1940, with his dog, Peter, and a reputation as one of the most fearless and skilful pilots in Fighter Command. In February 1941 he relinquished command of the Tiger Squadron to command the Biggin Hill Wing. At the same time his great friend Douglas Bader was appointed to lead the Tangmere Wing. (Photograph: Imperial War Museum)

5. RECONSTRUCTION

November 1940

BY dint of fantastic heroism, almost unequalled in history, the Luftwaffe hordes had been crippled and, in the process, a new name had arisen which symbolised to the whole country the bravery of its defenders — BIGGIN HILL. Already the tally had risen to record proportions and newspapers were acclaiming the heroic endurance of the young pilots of all squadrons who had been stationed on "The Bump".

There was little mention of the conditions under which everyone at Biggin Hill worked. Men and women were billetted in surrounding villages and the normal job of running the station was impossible. There were no proper offices and not even a nominal roll. On the North Camp not one building was intact apart from a disused Decontamination Centre and in there lived a solitary airman. He had taken shelter in the Centre during the bombing and stayed — claiming that as there was nothing left to bomb he was in the safest place.

The reconstruction of Biggin Hill began in November with repairs to Station Headquarters. When completed the administration staff moved in and found that it was far from adequate. The roof of the typists' office leaked and the staff had to walk a mile through mud for meals. On their first day back, six delayed-action bombs were dropped nearby and went off at intervals throughout the day.

Group Captain Grice and his assistant adjutant, Pilot Officer H.M. Leeming, needed help with the routine running of the station and it came in the form of Warrant Officer Gill who had been Trenchard's Flight Sergeant in the 1914-18 War. "Half Pint Gill" was blown off his bicycle by one of the explosions but accepted the experience with the wonderful *esprit de corps* which was a feature of the station in those difficult days.

During this time ground crews continued to work tirelessly day and night to keep the aerodrome serviceable and the aircraft flying. The WAAFs too, under the supervision of Assistant Section Officer Felicity Hanbury set an inspiring example although they were alarmed to learn that PT drill, abandoned after the bombing, was to be reinstated under the direction of Sergeant "Muscles" Freeman of the Sports and Welfare Section. In protest some of them threw their gym shoes in Keston Pond and claimed they could not exercise without them. "Muscles" disagreed.

After the bombing of Biggin the WAAFs were billetted in several large houses including this one close to the airfield. Another billet was at 'Cedars' in Keston village where there was a big scare when a German bomb missed the house by a few feet and embedded itself in the trunk of a magnificent old cedar tree outside with a muffled explosion. Some weeks later there was a crashing sound and the girls instinctively threw themselves on the floor. It was the old cedar — now laying prostrate — through delayed shock! (RAF Biggin Hill)

The pilots of 92 and 74 were now joined by 66 Squadron from West Malling and by the end of November the tally of enemy aircraft destroyed had reached 599. No other station in Fighter Command came within reach of this figure and there was great speculation over who would destroy the 600th Hun. Bets were taken all round and a large kitty grew for the fortunate pilot.

They hunted in two's

November 30, 1940

ON a cold, late November morning in 1940, with all squadrons grounded under a cloud base of something like 1,000 feet, two pilots casually climbed into their Spitfires and took off into the mist. The roar of the Merlin engines brought the whole station out to see who was crazy enough to fly in such weather. H.M. Stephen and Mungo Park had mutually decided to hunt and shoot down the station's 600th enemy aircraft.

Sailor Malan heard the Spitfires take off and with other pilots rushed to the Operations Room to follow the progress of his two flight commanders. He listened on the R/T as 11 Group HQ was told of the mission. An order came through immediately.

"O.K. Vector those two idiots to Deal. There's a convoy moving up Channel which might tempt Jerry — even in this weather".

Stephen and Mungo Park received their instructions and flew on towards their prey. A burst of Ack Ack fire from Deal sent them climbing higher and closer to a formation of eight Messerschmitts heading North. At 30,000 feet and well above a massive cloud cover, the German pilots must have been confident of a trouble free flight. Certainly Oberleutnant Schmidt, the "weaver" was unaware that two Spitfire pilots were closing in fast.

'We started to climb and climb and climb towards the German weaver. I opened with a two-second burst and broke away. I nipped in again and gave him three seconds from astern. I was overtaking too fast and broke away. Mungo got in again and overshot. I managed to get another ¼ deflection and raked him and overshot. E/A half rolled down and Mungo followed. Pilot forced down at Old Romney. Hermann Schmidt died 36 hours later.'

H.M. Stephen combat report

Pilot Officer Harbourne Mackay Stephen, aged 26 (right) and Flying Officer John Henry Mungo Park who believed in scrapping in two's. Park took command of 74 Squadron in March 1941 and in June of that year was shot down and killed. Stephen took command of 234 Squadron in July 1941 until 1942 when he was posted to the Far East. Later he commanded 166 fighter Wing.
(Imperial War Museum)

Pilot Officer H.M. Stephen took this photograph of his colleagues in 74 Squadron shortly after they arrived at Biggin Hill. They are (left to right): Sergeant Kirk, Flying Officer Franklin, Flying Officer Ricalton, Sergeant Ely, Flying Officer Boulding, ?,?,?, Pilot Officer Szczesny, Flight Lieutenant Malan, Flying Officer Mungo Park, Pilot Officer Draper, Flying Officer St. John, Sergeant Skinner, Pilot Officer Churches, Pilot Officer Chesters.

Farewell to Dickie Grice

December 1940

AFTER more than a year as Station Commander, Group Captain Grice left Biggin Hill with the tributes ringing in his ears. "If he had been a naval man", wrote Basil Cardew in the Daily Express, "his name would rank with the Harwoods and the Raleighs or, in the Army, with the Moores and the Allenbys.

"But the Group Captain leaves his beloved station as he came. To the public he will always be known as the anonymous RAF officer who commanded the 600 station".

"Groupie" Grice took leave of his men early in December, 1940 like the father of a boy who has scored a century on Founder's Day — pride covering his embarrassment. He was carried shoulder high by six fighter pilots through the Mess, and later that evening there was a great farewell party in the White Hart, Brasted.

It was one of many celebrations that winter. Sailor Malan won the DSO for "commanding his squadron with outstanding success". H.M. Stephen became the first recipient of a DSO awarded to a pilot officer in Great Britain. "Mungo" Park got the DFC while nine more DFCs and DFMs went to pilots of 74 and 92 Squadrons.

A veteran of the Royal Flying Corps, Group Captain F.O. Soden DFC, nicknamed "Mongoose" was the new Station Commander and his first duty was to write to the Secretary of State to the Air Ministry.

"I have just taken over Biggin Hill and the chaps are living under conditions of unnecessary filth and squalor; in fact: seldom, if ever, has so little been done for those few who have done so much for so many"!

The Air Ministry stepped up the reconstruction of RAF Biggin Hill.

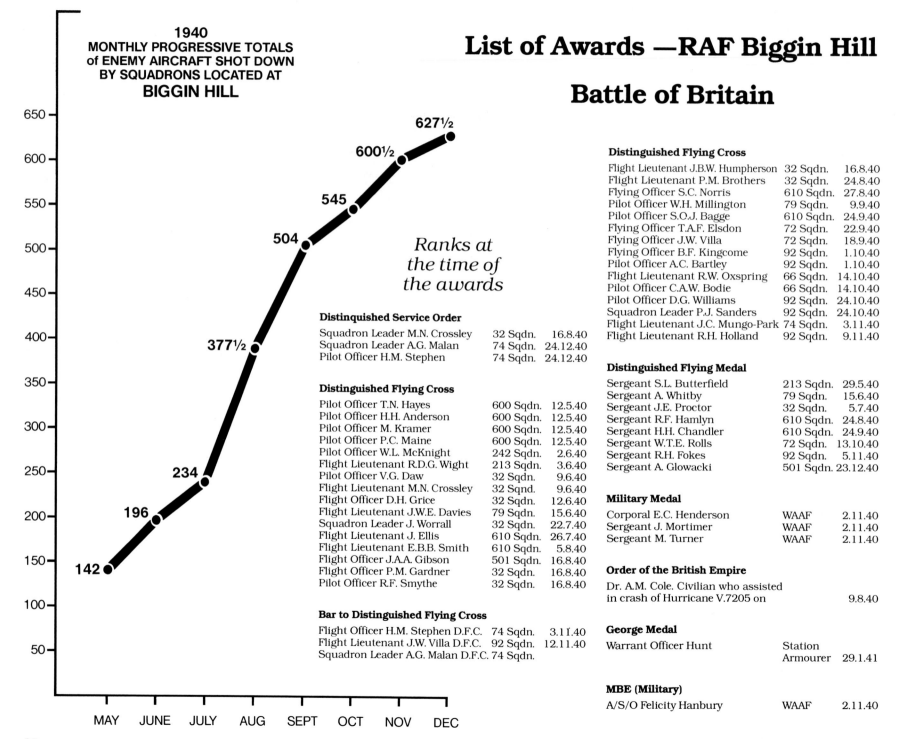

1940
MONTHLY PROGRESSIVE TOTALS of ENEMY AIRCRAFT SHOT DOWN BY SQUADRONS LOCATED AT BIGGIN HILL

Chart values: 142 (MAY), 196 (JUNE), 234 (JULY), 377½ (AUG), 504 (SEPT), 545 (OCT), 600½ (NOV), 627½ (DEC)

List of Awards —RAF Biggin Hill
Battle of Britain

Ranks at the time of the awards

Distinquished Service Order

Squadron Leader M.N. Crossley	32 Sqdn.	16.8.40
Squadron Leader A.G. Malan	74 Sqdn.	24.12.40
Pilot Officer H.M. Stephen	74 Sqdn.	24.12.40

Distinguished Flying Cross

Pilot Officer T.N. Hayes	600 Sqdn.	12.5.40
Pilot Officer H.H. Anderson	600 Sqdn.	12.5.40
Pilot Officer M. Kramer	600 Sqdn.	12.5.40
Pilot Officer P.C. Maine	600 Sqdn.	12.5.40
Pilot Officer W.L. McKnight	242 Sqdn.	2.6.40
Flight Lieutenant R.D.G. Wight	213 Sqdn.	3.6.40
Pilot Officer V.G. Daw	32 Sqdn.	9.6.40
Flight Lieutenant M.N. Crossley	32 Sqnd.	9.6.40
Flight Officer D.H. Grice	32 Sqdn.	12.6.40
Flight Lieutenant J.W.E. Davies	79 Sqdn.	15.6.40
Squadron Leader J. Worrall	32 Sqdn.	22.7.40
Flight Lieutenant J. Ellis	610 Sqdn.	26.7.40
Flight Lieutenant E.B.B. Smith	610 Sqdn.	5.8.40
Flight Officer J.A.A. Gibson	501 Sqdn.	16.8.40
Flight Officer P.M. Gardner	32 Sqdn.	16.8.40
Pilot Officer R.F. Smythe	32 Sqdn.	16.8.40

Bar to Distinguished Flying Cross

Flight Officer H.M. Stephen D.F.C.	74 Sqdn.	3.11.40
Flight Lieutenant J.W. Villa D.F.C.	92 Sqdn.	12.11.40
Squadron Leader A.G. Malan D.F.C.	74 Sqdn.	

Distinguished Flying Cross

Flight Lieutenant J.B.W. Humpherson	32 Sqdn.	16.8.40
Flight Lieutenant P.M. Brothers	32 Sqdn.	24.8.40
Flying Officer S.C. Norris	610 Sqdn.	27.8.40
Pilot Officer W.H. Millington	79 Sqdn.	9.9.40
Pilot Officer S.O.J. Bagge	610 Sqdn.	24.9.40
Flying Officer T.A.F. Elsdon	72 Sqdn.	22.9.40
Flying Officer J.W. Villa	72 Sqdn.	18.9.40
Flying Officer B.F. Kingcome	92 Sqdn.	1.10.40
Pilot Officer A.C. Bartley	92 Sqdn.	1.10.40
Flight Lieutenant R.W. Oxspring	66 Sqdn.	14.10.40
Pilot Officer C.A.W. Bodie	66 Sqdn.	14.10.40
Pilot Officer D.G. Williams	92 Sqdn.	24.10.40
Squadron Leader P.J. Sanders	92 Sqdn.	24.10.40
Flight Lieutenant J.C. Mungo-Park	74 Sqdn.	3.11.40
Flight Lieutenant R.H. Holland	92 Sqdn.	9.11.40

Distinguished Flying Medal

Sergeant S.L. Butterfield	213 Sqdn.	29.5.40
Sergeant A. Whitby	79 Sqdn.	15.6.40
Sergeant J.E. Proctor	32 Sqdn.	5.7.40
Sergeant R.F. Hamlyn	610 Sqdn.	24.8.40
Sergeant H.H. Chandler	610 Sqdn.	24.9.40
Sergeant W.T.E. Rolls	72 Sqdn.	13.10.40
Sergeant R.H. Fokes	92 Sqdn.	5.11.40
Sergeant A. Glowacki	501 Sqdn.	23.12.40

Military Medal

Corporal E.C. Henderson	WAAF	2.11.40
Sergeant J. Mortimer	WAAF	2.11.40
Sergeant M. Turner	WAAF	2.11.40

Order of the British Empire

Dr. A.M. Cole. Civilian who assisted in crash of Hurricane V.7205 on		9.8.40

George Medal

Warrant Officer Hunt	Station Armourer	29.1.41

MBE (Military)

A/S/O Felicity Hanbury	WAAF	2.11.40

In January 1941, 264 Squadron flew in from Gravesend with Defiants to make Biggin Hill its base for three months, before moving on to West Malling. Later the Defiants became non-operational and were replaced by Mosquitoes. (Photograph: RAF Biggin Hill)

Early in 1941, Jamie Rankin, a 28-year-old Scot replaced Johnny Kent as CO of 92 Squadron to the surprise and, in some cases, anger of the pilots. This was Rankin's first operational command and 92, of course, was the most successful squadron in Fighter Command. The Scot soon won the respect of his men for he was an outstanding pilot and a great shot. In fact he began to destroy Me109s with such regularity that he acquired the title — "One-a-day-Rankin".

Another pilot to make his operational debut at Biggin Hill with 92 Squadron was 19-year-old Neville Duke — one of the first fighter pilots to be trained in wartime. When Winston Churchill paid a visit to "The Bump", Duke tipped a Spitfire on to its nose as he came in to land — a faux pas that the Prime Minister chose to ignore. After the war, Duke became a household name for his incredible record-breaking performances as a Test Pilot. (Photographs: Imperial War Museum)

In February 1941, 609 (West Riding of Yorkshire) Squadron flew into Biggin Hill from Warmwell and the pilots were delighted to exchange Spitfire Is for Spitfire IIs. They were not so pleased to learn that their first operational flight, after three months of inactivity, was to take place the next day — an offensive sweep over France. The 609 Spitfire in the hangar was flown by Squadron Leader Michael Robinson. (RAF Biggin Hill)

In March, 1941, the three WAAFS who had been awarded the Military Medal — Sgt Elizabeth Mortimer, Corporal Elspeth Henderson and Sergeant Helen Turner — went to Buckingham Palace to collect their medals from the King. Naturally there was a celebration back at The Mess and the picture here shows, left to right: Polish pilot Henryk Szczesny; Group Captain Grice, Elizabeth Mortimer, Athol Forbes, Helen Turner, Johnny Kent, and officer from Group HQ. Seated: Free French pilot and Felicity Hanbury. Szczesny, with the KW and three bars, the VM (Fifth Class) and the DFC, had the distinction at one time of being the RAF's most bemedalled Flight Lieutenant. When this picture was taken Forbes was Commander of 66 Squadron which moved briefly from West Malling to Biggin Hill in November 1940. (Photograph: David Porter)

A blonde on his lap

April 1941

ONE of 92 Squadron's youngest pilots, 19-year-old Gordon Brettell, who always enjoyed the parties at Southwood when released from duty, decided one night he would take his girlfriend along. She was a WAAF, stationed at Tangmere.

Without permission from his CO, Brettell taxied off in his Spitfire, flew to Tangmere and returned with the girl on his lap. He touched down at Biggin Hill right in front of Group Captain Soden, who looked on with amazement as the hood slid back and a very pretty feminine blonde head appeared.

The young pilot was severely admonished and later court-martialled. His escapade, made him both infamous and a hero overnight. He was charged with endangering one of His Majesty's aircraft but refuted this and offered to repeat the feat either with the same girl or a dummy.

Pilot Officer Tony Bartley came to the rescue. In a statement he said he too had flown a Spitfire with a passenger and was prepared to do it again. There was nothing in the King's Regulations to say that a pilot and passenger should not fly in a single seater aircraft. The charge against Brettell was quashed.

Gordon Brettell, who was court-martialled for flying with a female in his Spitfire. Brettell was later shot down, captured and imprisoned in the notorious Stalag Luft III. He was among the RAF pilots murdered by the Gestapo after the mass break-out of March 1944.
(Photograph: Imperial War Museum)

A tragic return

April 1941

THE 'continental flavour' at Biggin Hill was enhanced considerably when Pilot Officer Comte Rudolphe Ghislain Charles de Hemricourt de Grunne made a distinguished return with the Belgian Flight of 609 Squadron. De Grunne had flown Hurricanes from "The Bump" with 32 Squadron but was shot down and spent a long period in hospital recovering from burns. He was sent on a special mission to Lisbon to find out what the German intentions were in East Africa. De Grunne's return to Biggin Hill was short. On May 25 1941 he escorted Blenheims on a raid to Bethune and was jumped by an Me109. He baled out into the sea. A rescue boat went out from Ramsgate but no trace of his body was found.

Squadron Leader de la Torre, known as "Spy" was the station's intelligence officer who would frequently brief the pilots before an operational flight and then insist they write their reports as soon as they returned. On some occasions the pilots were confused by new jargon which crept into their everyday language. Spy would always explain. He is pictured here, on the left. (Photograph: Imperial War Museum)

In the fashion now expected of them, the pilots of 92 East India Squadron celebrated their first anniversary on "The Bump" with a massive party and cabaret. Among the guests were Noel Coward pictured here with Wing Commander James Rankin and Miss Hambro. Biggin Hill was very popular with stage and screen stars. Laurence Olivier, Vivien Leigh and Jack Warner were frequent visitors. So was Jeanne de Casalis "Mrs Feather" of radio fame whose husband, Flight Lieutenant C.D. Stephenson was duty pilot officer. "Stevie" organised the exclusive PYFO club (Pull Your Finger Out) whose membership was accorded to those special friends of Biggin Hill. (Photograph: RAF Biggin Hill)

Uninjured in 300 sorties

A Sergeant Pilot posted to 92 Squadron some weeks after its arrival at "The Bump" was Don Kingaby (right), a vicar's son and former insurance official, who was to be known as "the 109 Specialist". With a score of 21 enemy aircraft destroyed, Kingaby became the top-scoring Sergeant in Fighter Command and was awarded three DFMs, the only man to be so honoured. Later he accepted a commission and won the DSO. This extraordinary pilot flew on more than 300 sorties during four years of fighting and was not once shot down or even injured, apart from a finger wound caused by a stray bullet as he walked away from his Spitfire at Manston.

(Photograph: Imperial War Museum)

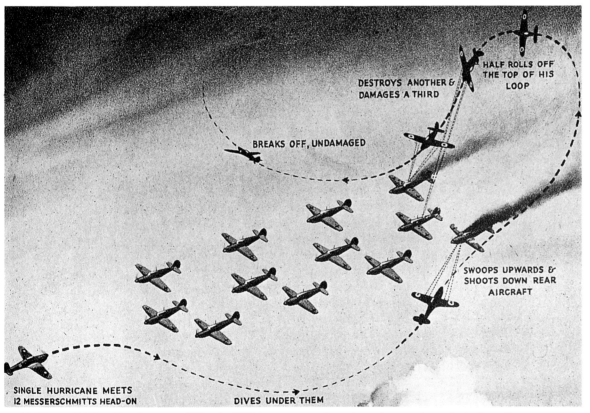

Seldom did the Hurricanes of Biggin Hill have any advantage in numbers, but often the enemy seemed unable to profit by his numerical superiority, although it must be remembered that the Germans, in 1940, were operating at a greater distance from their bases than were the British. Adolf Galland in his book, The First and Last wrote: "It used to take us roughly half an hour from take-off to cross the English coast at the narrowest part of the Channel. Having a tactical flying time of only 80 minutes, we therefore had about 20 minutes to complete our task . . ."

One tactic adopted by the British is explained in this diagram. A single Hurricane meeting 12 Messerschmitts head-on would dive under the formation, pick off tail-end Charlie, roll off the top of his loop, destroy a second and damage a third.

A piece of cake! Was it really? (Photograph: Ministry of Defence).

New legs for Bader

July 41

IN mid-summer of 1941, the Biggin Hill Wing took part in the "lean forward into France" as the offensive sweeps were called. Code named "Circus", bombers were used as bait to ensure the enemy came up and fought. The idea was to keep the Luftwaffe from comfortable contemplation of new objectives. Successes came almost every day but casualties were severe, particularly as far as 74 Squadron was concerned.

Peter Chesters of 74 Squadron was one pilot to die but in a rather unnecessary way. The Pilot Officer was so delighted to shoot down a Me109 that he executed his triumphant roll over the Manston station too low and crashed onto the parade ground killing himself instantly.

During the summer the fighter offensives increased and not a day passed without Biggin Hill Wing crossing the coast of France at least once. On "circus" operations the new four-engined Stirling bombers were used, each carrying 14 times the bomb load of a Blenheim. The escorting fighters from Biggin claimed the destruction of 50 enemy aircraft with 35 more "probables" in just a few weeks. Sailor Malan added six to his score and Jamie Rankin won the sweepstake for the squadron's 150th Hun.

609 Squadron also lost many pilots including its "heavenly twins" — Flight Lieutenant Churchin, shot down off Le Touquet and Pilot Officer Hill, killed a week later. There were miracles, too. Pilot Officer Malengrou, his engine knocked out by cannon fire, actually glided 20 miles back across the Channel, crash-landed in a hayfield and, in the Mess claimed the world's long distance gliding record for a single seater fighter!

At the end of July, 609 moved to Gravesend, and back to Biggin Hill came the Basutoland Squadron, No 72. On its first raid one aircraft had a very special mission — to drop a long wooden box onto St Omer airfield. The label on the box read: "Dieser Kasten enhalt Beinprothese fur Wing Commander Douglas Bader, RAF Kriegsgefangener".

"Tinlegs" Bader was a POW and Adolf Galland, commanding the Geschwader had arranged for an aircraft to drop, by parachute, a spare set of artificial limbs.

Squadron Leader Douglas Bader, probably the best-known fighter pilot in the Battle of Britain. (Photograph: Imperial War Museum)

'Mongoose' and 'The Midget'

June-July 1941

Group Captain Dickie Barwell, the station commander who loved to fly with the Wing, taxied off and, over the valley to the west of Biggin Hill, his Spitfire engine cut out and he made a desperate crash landing into a field. Barwell was dragged from the wreckage with a broken vertebrae and taken to hospital where his spine was encased in plaster. Two weeks later, he was back at work, flying and collecting autographs from some of the stage and screen personalities who visited the Mess. (Pictured here signing his plaster cast is Jeanne de Casalis). (Photograph: RAF Biggin Hill)

A unique plan to introduce another pair of eyes in a Spitfire formation was sent to the Air Ministry by Group Captain Soden who was alarmed by the increasing number of losses. Writing about his idea at the time, the Station Commander said: "The backward view from a Spitfire was bad and our formations, in spite of continual weaving, were being jumped. I felt that if we could have even one pair of eyes looking aft we might avoid more losses.

"We got to work on a damaged Spitfire and found that if we sacrificed one gun and ammo on each side it would be possible to make room for the R/T from behind the pilot and fit a very small seat for a midget from a circus.

"I showed my mock-up to Prof. Sir Henry Tizard and he asked for photographs and a write-up of my idea to be sent to the Air Ministry. It was not long before the balloon went up. I was summoned to Fighter Command where I received the biggest raspberry of all time by the Chief of Staff for short-circuiting Fighter Command.

"That was the end of that".

And that was the end of "Mongoose" Soden at Biggin Hill. His place as CO was taken in June, 1941 by Group Captain Philip Barwell, a man who preferred flying with his Wing to the routine duties of administration.

Unconscious in the sky

August 1941

ACTING Squadron Leader Ken Campbell of 72 Squadron was returning from a fighter sweep in August 1941 when he spotted the yellow stain, released when a pilot bales out into the sea. Despite the presence of enemy aircraft in the area, Ken alerted the rescue launch by a May Day call, pinpointed the pilot's exact position and circled the spot for a few minutes. Some days later he repeated the action and was immediately recommended for a DFC.

A few months later he was involved in a sweep over Le Touquet when German fighters popped out of the clouds. Weaving out of the way a Spitfire crashed into his tail and cut it off. Campbell takes up the story: "My stick and rudder control went dead, the aircraft still climbing, lost speed and fell over into a spin. My estimated height was 21,000 feet. Remembering my last emergency exit from a Hurricane, I undid my sutton harness, released my R/T cable and my oxygen tube and grasped the rubber ball at the end of a chain which jettisoned the hood.

"I pulled so hard that the rubber ball came off the chain, but the hood was still in place. The aircraft was spinning madly, but that hardly registered. Using all my strength I was too intent on releasing the hood. Suddenly it went and I felt the slipstream pouring into the cockpit.

"I attempted to stand to get out of the cockpit, but failed, the pressure was forcing me back. I could not get out. I realised I was in a centripetal spin and passed into unconsciousness through lack of oxygen".

Campbell awakened to find himself falling through the air in a sitting position. He released his parachute and went into the sea about a mile from the French coast. He began to swim and was rescued by a French fishing boat which took him ashore. Campbell was arrested and became a prisoner of war.

Ken Campbell could be giving the Churchill "victory" salute but, in fact, he's showing Pilot Officer Naeyer and Sergeant Watson of 72 Squadron the sign for "wheels down".

A funeral cortége moves slowly along Star Lane, St Mary Cray, with pall-bearers carrying the coffin of a 20 year-old Pilot Officer, William Watling, who was killed on February 7, 1941. Watling, who was with 92 Squadron for all of his eight months as a fighter pilot, was buried with full military honours in the Star Lane Cemetery alongside Flying Officer James Paterson, Flight Sergeant Charles Sydney, Squadron Leader Joseph O'Brien and many of those killed in the bombing of Biggin Hill. (see page 129).
(Photograph: N. T. Freeman)

Chief of the Guinea Pigs

THERE were many good drinking sessions during the war in which the participants solemnly arranged to meet regularly and remain a band of brothers. Most of them faded with the next-day's hangover. The party held at Ward Three of the Queen Victoria Hospital, East Grinstead on July 19, 1941 was different, for a group of airmen conceived an idea for a club that was officially formed the following day. Forty nine years later it is still flourishing.

It is The Guinea Pig Club and its members are those airmen who were severely or partially "fried" in their aircraft during the war and have undergone plastic surgery. Ward Three, in 1941, was a little brown wooden army hut behind the main hospital building where the brilliant surgeon, Archie McIndoe, grafted new skin on the hands, faces and bodies of the terribly burned victims of Dunkirk and the Battle of Britain.

One of the patients at that inaugural meeting was Tom Gleave who was elected vice-president of the Guinea Pig Club (McIndoe was President). Tom was in Ward Three being fitted with a new nose and undergoing other surgery to his face, hands and legs. His story is typical of the painful experience of hundreds of young pilots.

Squadron Leader Tom Gleave, on August 31, 1940 was the officer commanding 253 Squadron based at Kenley and he was leading an attack on a formation of Junkers 88s, Dornier 17s and Heinkel 111s, heading for Biggin Hill. Tom formulated his attacks in a series of barrel rolls from beneath the enemy, consistently pressing them home until he could see the features of his adversaries, but the aerial combat resulted in irreparable damge to his Hurricane, fire rapidly engulfing the cockpit. Tom had no alternative but to attempt to bale out.

He reached down to pull the radio telephone lead out of its socket but the heat was too great and with skin burning off his right hand he could not muster the strength to obtain the leverage required. The chance of survival was now measured in seconds and he knew his only means of escape was to rip off his helmet and oxygen mask and expose his head and face to the inferno. As he opened the cockpit cover the now inverted aircraft exploded and he was thrown clear.

Tom's Irvin parachute had miraculously received only slight damage and he descended into a field adjoining Mace Farm, Cudham, Kent. During his descent he realised he was still holding his parachute rip-cord release handle and, although it had become fused to the skin, through his burnt gloves he hurled it away.

Tom Gleave's Hurricane which had been 'lost' in all but memory by the constantly maturing woodland was eventually located in 1967 by members of the Flairavia Flying Club. The engine was transported to Biggin Hill by a farmer and, at that time, was the only battle Merlin known to exist. Picture shows Tom Gleave (right) in the woodlands close to the spot where his Hurricane crashed.

Unable to see clearly, burnt skin from his forehead having fallen across his eyes, with his hands and legs burnt and ripped open exposing to the bone, he collided with the ground with considerable impact. He stumbled towards a gate where the farmer Mr Wilson and his son were running towards him.

Tom was now to begin 11 months in hospital at first in Orpington and then East Grinstead, where Archie McIndoe sculptured a new nose. The skin for his nose came from his forehead. The skin for his forehead came from his thigh. Eventually Tom left hospital to continue with a distinguished career in the RAF, returning frequently to hospital for further plastic surgery.

Group Captain Gleave retired with awards given by Britain, France, America and Belgium but his greatest honour of all was that of Chief Guinea Pig. In this capacity he has devoted his time unceasingly to the well-being of 650 airmen, including many who flew from Biggin Hill, who are members of one of the most exclusive clubs in the world.

Tom Gleave calls his injuries "standard Hurricane burns". He received them in defending "The Bump" — in an action that is an integral part of the station's history.

David Porter

Where is Vicky? In the drink!

September — October 1941

THE extraordinary reshuffling of Squadrons between Biggin Hill, West Malling, Gravesend and Manston continued throughout the summer of 1941 but in September, 92 Squadron left "The Bump" never to return. They exchanged places with 609 and moved into the grand Elizabethan Manor at Cobham Hall near Gravesend. A few weeks later they were ordered to Digby.

The Basutoland Squadron, 72, also left and the Royal Canadian Air Force flew in to Biggin Hill with their crack 401 Squadron.

The pilots of 609 were pleased to be back. They were now the senior squadron and had enjoyed an extraordinary run of success. Among their numbers was a wonderful Belgium pilot, Vicky Ortmans DFC, C de G(Belg) who had escaped to England in 1940 after his squadron had been completely wiped out at Liege.

Ortmans was a pilot who "enjoyed a swim". On five occasions he came down in the "drink" and

was rescued twice by the same launch. In the Mess the boys would frequently discuss Vicky's passion for plunging into the Channel from 20,000 feet or even more.

On October 21, the day that his younger brother Christian made his operational debut, Vicky Ortmans was shot down again, somewhere over Boulogne. The squadron searched the sea expecting to find their hero, as usual, waving from a dinghy. There was no sign of him. This time Vicky was lost.

The Belgian had in fact gone down in flames again. Badly wouded he baled out into the sea and managed to inflate his dinghy. For two days and a night Ortmans bobbed up and down in the Channel but the boys never appeared. This time they had left him for dead. Eventually Vicky was beached near Dieppe and taken prisoner.

Ortman's luck finally ran out in 1948 when he was killed in a flying accident.

Farewell 92

The figures on the board speak for themselves. This is the 1940 tally for 92 East India Squadron, which included some of the highest scoring aces in Fighter Command. On September 21, 1941 with considerably more successes, the "92 Foot and Mouth" said goodbye to "The Bump". L to R: Flight Lieutenant Harland, Tom Weiss the Norwegian Intelligence Officer, Pilot Officer Roy Mottram, Sergeant "Tich" Havercroft, Flight Lieutenant Brian Kingcome, Squadron Leader Johnny Kent, Flying Officer Thomas "Jock" Sherrington, Pilot Officer Cecil "Fishy" Saunders, Flying Officer Bob Holland, Pilot Officer Alan Wright, Sergeant Hugh Bowen-Morris, Flying Officer Tommy Lund.

(Photograph: Imperial War Museum)

For two days and one night Vicky Ortmans bobbed up and down in his dinghy. (Photograph: South Eastern Newspapers Ltd)

Many pilots failed to return. Some made it back to Biggin — but only just. This Supermarine Spitfire VB of 401 Squadron of the Royal Canadian Air Force, whose pilots arrived in September 1941, force -landed at Biggin Hill on October 23, 1941.

American award

Squadron Leader Raymond Duke-Woolley, who commanded 124 flew in to Biggin Hill on November 17, 1941 with one of the most cosmopolitan squadrons ever assembled. Its pilots included Belgians, French, Czechoslovakians, Norwegians, Australians and Canadians. They came to join the New Zealanders, Poles and British and commanding the Wing was a South African. The Eagles were yet to arrive but Duke-Woolley was a man who was to make a great impression with the Americans. In January 1943 he was posted to the 8th USAAF Bomber Command as Fighter Liaison Officer and became the only non-American to win the US DFC. He is pictured above receiving the award from Lieutenant Colonel C.G. Peterson, then a former Commander of the Eagles. (Photograph: John Freeman)

He thrived on action

December 17, 1941

AS the end of the second full year of the war approached there were many changes at Biggin Hill. Sailor Malan had already left on a special mission to the United States and the Wing, having been led for a while by Michael Robinson, had a vacancy for a new leader. Jamie Rankin, soon to leave for a training post at HQ became Commander of Flying and handed 92 over to Dickie Milne, a young Scot.

The station was delighted when they heard who was to be the new Wingco — Robert Stanford Tuck, a splendidly unflappable and brilliant young officer who had already made his mark with Fighter Command and thrived on action. Bobby Tuck was well known at Biggin Hill and, indeed, at the White Hart in Brasted where he frequently dropped in for a pint with his old friends.

Kath Preston, the landlady, often wondered why German Intelligence had not identified her pub for a specific bombing raid. On a Saturday night towards closing time they could have wiped out a complete squadron and saved themselves a lot of trouble. Tuck understood her nervousness.

Just over a year earlier he was enjoying a drink with his future wife Joyce and some of the boys at the Ferry Inn near Coltishall, Norfolk where he was stationed with 257 Squadron. He suddenly jumped up and said: "Let's go to Norwich". Grabbing Joyce's arm, he led her out to the car and explained that he had no desire to go to Norwich but felt an urge to get away from Ferry Inn which he couldn't explain.

Next morning a pilot told him the news. Just before the bell rang for last orders, the inn had received a direct hit from a lone German raider. Six were killed and several injured.

On January 28, 1942 Tuck was given an "alcoholic" target — the distillery at Hesdin, inland from Le Touquet. He found the giant vats, pumped cannon shells into them and looked around for more excitement. A locomotive lured him into the sights of the flak defences at Boulogne and Tuck's Spitfire was trapped in the crossfire. He made a heavy forced landing in a field and was taken prisoner.

His place was taken by Wing Commander Masterman.

Robert Stanford Tuck who survived more hair-raising adventures in the war than most. On August 25, 1940 Tuck's Spitfire was so badly damaged that he glided 15 miles and made a forced landing on a dead engine. (Photograph: Imperial War Museum)

The Eagles have landed

May 3, 1942

THE "Old Glory" was unfurled at Biggin Hill on May 3, 1942 by the pilots of the Third Eagle Squadron, 133, who flew in that morning from Kirton Lindsey where they had been trained on Spitfires.

These American volunteers in the Royal Air Force were longing for action. To them Biggin Hill was in the heart of the "big flap country", just a few miles across the water from the Nazi menace — and some dangerously exciting missions.

Junior of the three Eagle squadrons, 133 was formed at Eglington shortly before the United States entered the war. The Americans were all civilians with a love of flying and they came to England in search of adventure from 13 States.

Among those at Biggin Hill was Don Blakeslee who had flown with the Canadian 401 Squadron and had more experience than any other pilot in the group. He was due "for a rest" and, fearful he would be taken off combat duty, asked for a transfer to the Eagles. Flight Commanders were "Cobey" King, a former Hollywood stunt pilot and "Red" McColpin who was to earn the reputation as the most dangerous poker player on "The Bump". Four pilots came from one town in California. They were dubbed "Four Horsemen of the Apocalypse".

The Americans quickly found a pub of their own. The Queen's Head at Downe where they played darts, shove ha'penny, sang their battle song and looked forward to meeting the Hun in combat.

The first few operations were uneventful but the poker player, McColpin, dealt the first blow for the Eagles by sending down one Me109 and claiming two probables.

This operational experience was to prove valuable for "The Big Show" — the Dieppe raid timed for August 19, 1942. The Eagles moved to Lympne with 401 Squadron and two fresh Squadrons, 222 and 602, flew into Biggin Hill, the latter commanded by Squadron Leader Peter Brothers making a return to "The Bump".

With the rest of the Biggin Hill Wing these squadrons provided a fighter "umbrella" over Dieppe while some 6,000 troops attempted to destroy all military installations. After several patrols the score was five enemy aircraft destroyed, seven probables and 29 damaged. Six Spitfires were lost.

In September the Eagles became part of the 4th Fighter Group of the US Eighth Army and, sadly, said goodbye to "The Bump".

May 3, 1942 — the New World joins the Old World on "The Bump".
(Photograph: Imperial War Museum)

The blackout screen

DURING late 1941 and early 1942 five squadrons came and left Biggin Hill — and each pilot had his favourite pub.

Sergeant Hughes of 72 Squadron liked the King's Arms at Leaves Green. Returning home after destroying an Me109, his own Spitfire badly damaged, Hughes landed without flaps or brakes. He ran along the entire length of the runway, across the perimeter track, over a new extension being built and came to a halt near the public bar of the King's Arms. Hughes stepped out and ordered a pint of bitter!

The pilots of 609 Squadron preferred The Jail at Biggin Hill where the jolly landlady presented them with their mascot, Wing Commander William B. Goat. When 609 moved base William Goat went with them.

The Americans adopted the Queen's Head at Downe as their local and would often cycle down the long steep hill that led into the village.

No pilot, however, could stay away from the White Hart at Brasted for long and when their former Station Commander Group Captain Grice was posted overseas to Australia, a great farewell party was planned.

During the evening Dickie Grice signed his name on the blackout screen in the pub and encouraged his former colleagues to add their signatures. Brian Kingcome, Al Deere, Jamie Rankin, Sailor Malan, Dickie Milne, Tony Bartley and Johnny Johnson, who had joined the party, were among the first names on the board.

Others were added in later years and the board became one of the country's best-known memorials to "The Few". Today it has pride of place in the RAF Museum at Hendon.

The first of the Few on the famous blackout screen in The White Hart. (Photograph: Kath Preston)

This photograph of Bob Stanford Tuck and Roger Bushell, looking rather dishevelled, was taken at the notorious prisoner of war camp, Stalag Luft III. Bushell became OC Escaping and was murdered on May 28, 1944 with 46 other airmen after they had tunnelled their way from the "escape-proof" prison in Silesia. Tuck managed to escape — from a different POW camp. He was found by the Russians in mid-February 1945 and spent two weeks fighting alongside them. Tuck eventually reached the British Embassy in Moscow and was put on a ship for Southampton. (Photograph: Imperial War Museum)

Shot down — by a Spitfire

July 1, 1942

DURING the spring of 1942, 25 Allied aircraft were shot down by Allied fighters, a frightening situation which prompted Group Captain Barwell and "Spy" de la Torre to hold identification competitions at Biggin Hill. They wanted their pilots to recognise the new Hurricanes and Spitfires, the Typhoons and Mosquitoes, now being flown daily, the Bostons, Baltimores, Tomahawks, Marylands and Mustangs from America.

Barwell knew that, in combat, there was no time to consult an aircraft manual. His men must learn. He wanted no mistakes from the pilots of Biggin Hill.

The Group Captain was still in plaster and had great difficulty in turning his head but he still flew regularly on patrols, usually Red Two to Squadron Leader Duke Woolley. On July 1, 1942 Barwell took off with Squadron Leader Bobby Oxspring in a Spitfire V1, a high altitude version with extended wings. The pilots were on a mission to hunt down a lone reconnaissance aircraft which had been seen over Beachy Head. Unknown to Barwell or Oxspring two more Spitfires took off from Tangmere to hunt the same Hun.

Over the Channel there was no sign of the German. The Tangmere pilots, however, spotted an unfamiliar fighter and dived. Bursts of machine gun fire were directed at Dickie Barwell's Spitfire which spun down in flames. Hampered by his plaster cast and unable to free himself, the man with the broken back crashed into the sea. The Controller at Biggin Hill radioed Tangmere. "I think your boys have shot down our station commander".

The whole station was aware of the tragic irony. Dickie Barwell, the man with a fetish for aircraft identification, had been shot down . . . by a Spitfire.

HUGO Armstrong and "Timber" Woods, Flight Commanders of 72 Squadron were the first pilots from Biggin Hill to fly the new Spitfire IX. Powered by Rolls Royce Merlin engines the new Spitfire was vastly superior to the Mark Vs and equal to the Focke-Wulf 190. The Spitfire IX had a four-blade airscrew, two rads under the wings, a long range tank under the centre section and was formidably armed with two cannon and four more guns. Armstrong and Woods were certainly impressed. They reported an air speed of 480 mph in a shallow dive at 25,000 feet. 72 Squadron was re-equipped.

Group Captain "Dickie" Barwell welcomes HRH The Duke of Kent to Biggin Hill. Within a few days both men had been killed — the Duke of Kent in a flying accident, Barwell shot down by a Spitfire. (Photograph: RAF Biggin Hill)

12 Spitfires lost

September 1942

THE first Free French Squadron to be based at Biggin Hill was Le Groupe, Ile de France, No 340 Squadron. They arrived in mid-September 1942 shortly after the American Eagles — and were looking forward to flying the new Mark IX Spitfires.

They were unlucky. On their final mission from Biggin Hill the Eagle pilots were blown 100 miles off course by a vicious head wind and when they emerged from the clouds they found themselves at Brest, not Cornwall as they had expected. The flak defences in this heavily-guarded French Port opened up and all 12 Mark IX Spitfires were badly holed. Eleven landed and the pilots were taken prisoner by the Luftwaffe. The twelfth tried to make it back to Cornwall and crashed onto the cliffs of The Lizard.

A solemn occasion for 340 Squadron came on November 10 when General de Gaulle visited Biggin Hill and inspected the pilots and ground crews. During lunch that followed in the Mess, de Gaulle told them that preparations were in hand for the liberation of France.

General de Gaulle at Biggin Hill on November 10, 1942. On the left is Group Captain Hallings-Pott DSO AFC who had taken over as Station Commander following the death of 'Dickie' Barwell. (Photograph: Imperial War Museum)

Spitfire IXs of 611 Squadron fly low over the Salt Box towards Bromley on December 9, 1942. The walls are all that remain of the triple-bay hangar blown up by Group Captain Grice in 1940. Behind the hangar is the cupola of the station headquarters. In front is a 40mm Bofors AA gun and the Nissen huts and sheds used for maintenance and dispersal. 611 West Lancs Squadron had arrived on September 23 for a three-month stay on "The Bump" (Photograph Imperial War Museum)

As 340 Ile de France Squadron takes off on January 19, 1943 for a daylight sweep, a critical audience of fighter pilots and mechanics watch from the top of an air raid shelter. (Photograph: Imperial War Museum)

Sailor Malan, DSO and Bar, DFC and Bar, Belgian Croix de Guerre, the top scoring ace in Fighter Command, took over "Britain's Number One Fighter Station" in a blaze of publicity. Group Captain Hallings-Pott, who had run the show since Dickie Barwell's untimely death, had left and the Sailor was back to lift morale, which in January 1943 was as soggy as the weather. Malan is pictured here with an all Dominion cast, Jack Charles of Canada (centre) and Al Deere of New Zealand. (Photograph: Imperial War Museum)

Desperate Days

March 1943

FOR several weeks the boys at "The Bump" looked forward to the evening of March 23, 1943 and all the gaiety and glamour which the Windmill Girls provided during their occasional visits to the camp theatre. Sadly, it was cancelled at the last moment after one of Biggin Hill's blackest days. Dickie Milne, Wing Commander Flying developed engine trouble near Hardelot and was shot down by Focke-Wulf 190s. He was taken prisoner. Wing Commander Slater, a newcomer to Biggin Hill and Commandant Reilhac, CO of 340 Squadron, the first French unit to be stationed there, were also "bounced" in the same "rodeo" and failed to return to base.

Squadron Leader Hugo Armstrong, CO of 611 Squadron was another "veteran" pilot to lose his life. He set off on a routine practice flight over the Channel on February 5, 1943 and joined 340 Squadron who were on a patrol. Flying under the clouds the Spitfires were surprised by eight Huns off Boulogne and as Armstrong went down in flames he was heard to say: "This is it chaps, I'm baling out". Despite a long search he was never seen again.

Dickie Milne — shot down by FW 190s.

Hugo Armstrong — never seen again.

The man with nine lives

February 1943

FLIGHT Lieutenant Alan Deere DFC, a 23-year-old New Zealander, known as the champion baler-out or the man "Germans couldn't kill" took over as Wing Commander Flying at Biggin Hill and began an eventful partnership with his great friend, Sailor Malan.

Deere, who had used his parachute more times than any other Spitfire pilot, already had 22 confirmed victories and a great number of adventures. In 1940 during a dawn patrol his glycol tank was holed and he force-landed on a beach, knocking himself unconscious. Coming to, Deere climbed out of his burning aircraft and made his way to Dunkirk in a series of abandoned cars and one bicycle. After a long wait on the beaches he managed to get a destroyer back to Dover, a train to London, an underground to Hornchurch, where he was stationed, and was ready for action next day.

Six weeks later Deere had a head-on collision with an Me109. With his cockpit hood jammed he managed to keep his blazing Hurricane in the air for another five minutes, then crashed, slithered along the ground and was stopped by a tree. Deere broke the perspex with his hands and calmly stepped out.

On August 15, 1941, Deere had to bale out very low after being chased across the Channel by two enemy fighters. He fractured his wrist. On the 30th he was one of three Spitfire pilots caught in a bombing attack on Hornchurch. His aircraft was thrown on its back and he was left suspended in his harness. He was rescued by a pilot with leg injuries.

He also had a great sense of humour. A story told by his Kiwi colleague Johnny Checketts concerns the day he was returning from a sweep over France when the voice of "Mitzi" Darling, who was flying nearby, sounded in his earphone. "Are you alright, Deere?". Al didn't hesitate. "Yes, Darling", he replied.

Sailor's Ten Commandments

SAILOR Malan's first act as Commander was to draw up a list of his ten rules for air fighting — Malan's Ten Commandments. They were posted up in The Mess and in dispersal huts and were soon in great demand by fighter stations all over the country. The new roles helped morale to soar, for the whole of Biggin Hill knew that the station commander was a man who practised what he preached when it mattered. (Photograph: RAF Biggin Hill)

TEN of MY RULES for AIR FIGHTING

1. Wait until you <u>see the whites of his eyes.</u>
   Fire short bursts of 1 to 2 seconds and only when your sights are definitely 'ON'.

2. Whilst shooting think of nothing else, brace the whole of the body; have both hands on the stick; concentrate on your ring sight.

3. Always keep a sharp lookout. "Keep your finger out"!

4. Height gives <u>You</u> the initiative.

5. Always turn and face the attack.

6. Make your decisions promptly. It is better to act quickly even though your tactics are not the best.

7. Never fly straight and level for more than 30 seconds in the combat area.

8. When diving to attack always leave a proportion of your formation above to act as top guard.

9. INITIATIVE, AGGRESSION, AIR DISCIPLINE. and TEAM WORK are words that MEAN something in Air Fighting.

10. Go in quickly — Punch hard — Get out!

1,000 kills — the honour is shared *May 15, 1943*

ONE rousing event in the Spring of 1943 gripped the imagination of the whole country and confirmed Biggin Hill's status as the major battle ground of the RAF and the castle keep in the defence of London and the south east. The sector claimed its 1000th enemy plane to be shot down.

The story leading up to this achievement began on March 11 when a fighting Frenchman called "Rene" Moved to "The Bump" with his 341 Alsace Squadron. "Rene" Mouchotte dared only to fight under a pseudonym for fear of reprisals against his family in occupied France.

On the eve of his squadron's move to Biggin Hill, "Rene" forecast: "The day of the offensive which is fast approaching will find a young force, terribly armed with a science of warfare and discipline. We shall put our whole soul into this holy war of liberation and the Octopus shall perish, even if it costs us our lives. . . .

A few weeks later Sailor Malan spoke to the whole station. "You are members of the Sector Station which has produced the most outstanding achievements in the Battle of Britain and which, not being content with the standards set in 1940, has continued in the lead as the foremost sector in this Command.

"Today, as most of you know, the Biggin Hill Sector is closely approaching its thousandth confirmed victory, not to mention the "probably confirmed" and "unconfirmed. . . . . . .

"Every minute of every day you spend at your work you are performing a task which is making history and which will go down to posterity as the most glorious achievement by a magnificent Service at a time when its country and Empire needed it most".

The thousandth Hun? Who was going to shoot it down? Everyone was gripped by feverish expectancy. A sweepstake was organised with £300 for the successful pilot and £150 for the win-

ner. Newspaper reporters kept in touch with Biggin Hill daily. Mr Gilbert Harding, a BBC interviewer, prepared a recording of the great occasion.

On May 7, Squadron Leader Jack Charles, the Canadian CO of 611 Squadron, Sergeant Clark, also of 611 and Martell of 341 took the tally to 998 and everyone waited for the next fine day. It came on May 15 when Alan Deere announced: "An easy one, chaps. Just a quickie over Caen". In the Operations Room there was a clamour for "ringside" seats as the Spitfires took off and everyone waited for Deere to speak again: "Brutus aircraft, look out! Bandits climbing at 3 o'clock". A pack of Focke-Wulfs were about to attack a formation of Bostons which the Biggin Hill Squadrons were escorting across the Channel.

The Controller at Biggin Hill, Bill Igoe remained calm and cheerful but everyone else was fidgeting nervously as Jack Charles took 611 into a vertical dive in the "Malan formation" of four-in-a-line astern. Mouchotte and his Alsace pilots gave cover as Charles quickly gained the 999th, rolled, turned, climbed and fixed a second FW190 in his gunsight.

As the Canadian prepared to fire Mouchotte, above, saw another 190 under his starboard wing. He gave chase and stabbed the button in complete unison with Charles. Two Huns fell from the sky.

Biggin Hill had come a long way since a boy called Jimmy Davies shot down a Dornier 17 way back in 1939. The station total now stood at 1,001 — but who could claim the thousandth, Mouchotte or Charles? Sailor Malan with great diplomacy ruled that they should share the honour and Biggin Hill was besieged with newsreel cameramen and radio reporters.

A Frenchman and a Canadian were the heroes of England.

Squadron Leader Jack Charles and Commandant 'René' Mouchotte —
they shared the 1000th. (Photograph: Imperial War Museum)

125

'ONE CONFIRMED'!

BILL HOOPER
R.A.F
43

This cartoon drawn by Bill Hooper has hung in the Officers' Mess for almost 50 years. It shows Jack Charles (left) and Rene Mouchotte claiming their prize 1000 with some encouragement from Sailor Malan (with the anchor) and Al Deere (by the throat) The Intelligence Officer "Spy" de la Torre is keeping the score.

The greatest party yet

May 1943

BIGGIN Hill had organised many brilliant parties but the greatest ever was the one to celebrate the thousandth kill in May 1943. It was held at Grosvenor House, a glittering venue, and attended by 1,000 guests.

Air Chief Marshals Sir Trafford Leigh Mallory of Fighter Command and Sir Arthur Harris of Bomber Command were there. So were all the available pilots of 11 Group, the officers of Biggin Hill, stage and screen stars and politicians. Vivian Van Dam of The Windmill Theatre provided a glamorous cabaret and the food was so mouthwatering it was easy to forget this was the middle of a war.

The top table was adorned by joints of beef, chicken and three large lobsters named Hitler, Mussolini and Goebbels. In front of the gallery along one wall of the ballroom was a full-scale model of a Spitfire giving the impression of banking out of a cloud as the light from the gallery played on to it. The bar was free and three RAF bands provided the music.

A memento of that party still survives in the Officers' Mess at Biggin Hill. It is the steering wheel of a cab. Fifty London cabbies insisted on driving the pilots up to Grosvenor House free of charge for the thousandth kill night. The steering wheel is inscribed: "From the boys in the cabs to the boys we had the honour to drive".

In return for their help, Malan invited the cabbies to be his guests of honour at Biggin Hill. Cabman Barney Dowling composed a song which everyone, gloriously intoxicated, sang outside the Mess.

One of the 50 London cabbies who drove the pilots to Grosvenor House free of charge. Meanwhile the Operations Section was organising its own celebration party for "the pranging of 1000 Hun planes". This ticket belongs to Doug Geer who was at the party.

Admit Two

4

R.A.F. STATION — BIGGIN HILL

OPERATIONS SECTION

CELEBRATION PARTY
to commemorate the pranging of
1000 HUN PLANES
at
THE ROOKERY, BROMLEY COMMON
on
Thursday, 29th July, 1943

From 8.30 to ? ? ?   Refreshments, Dancing

Here's to the lads of Biggin Hill,
Who gave us many a thrill,
When things look glum,
Now we'd got them on the run,
When they fly from Biggin Hill,
Led by Sailor Malan and
His merry band....

Soon after the death of "Rene" Mouchotte, a little memorial chapel was established in a disused army hut and dedicated by Sailor Malan on September 19, 1943. (Photograph: RAF Biggin Hill) see page 143.

'I am alone with the Bombers'

BIGGIN Hill featured prominently in the diary of "Rene" Mouchotte, the fighting Frenchman. Here are some of the entries:

March 17, 1943

The incredible signal came yesterday evening. We are moving south to relieve and replace old 340 at Biggin Hill. My boys are wild with delight. Martel and Farman who came to England together after crossing Spain on foot simply cannot contain themselves.

July 27, 1943

The other Squadron in the Wing got four which makes nine altogether, perhaps more, without loss. A considerable success which will further exalt our Alsace. I received telegrams of congratulations, one of them from Winston Churchill as follows: 'Please convey my warmest congratulations to 341 and 485 Squadrons on yesterday's achievement. Nine for nought is an excellent score.'

July 27, 1943 (later entry)

The sweeps go on at a terrible pace. I am at the record figure of 140. I feel a pitiless weariness from them. It is useless for me to go to bed at 9.30 each night; I feel my nerves wearing out, my temper deteriorating. The smallest effort gets me out of breath; I have a crying need for a rest, were it even for 48 hours.

One month later the Alsace Squadron, with Mouchotte leading, flew off on a raiding mission with Flying Fortresses. They were attacked by Focke-Wulfs diving out of the sun. In another desperate life or death fight, Mouchotte's voice came over the R/T. "I am alone with the bombers". He was never seen again.

Sailor Malan spoke at "Rene's" funeral. "He was a leader, a fighter and a gentleman. We shall miss him".

The Star Lane Cemetery at St. Mary Cray where the bodies of many of those killed in the bombing of Biggin Hill in 1940 are interred. Alongside them are a few young pilots. See page 109.

SQUADRONS AT BIGGIN HILL 1918-1958

PRINCIPAL UNITS

From	Date	Unit	Aircraft	Mark	Code	Date	To
Rochford	8.2.18	141	Bristol Fighters Mixed collection			1.3.19	Tailaght
Stow Marries	17.3.19	37 renumbered39	Snipes			18.1.22	Kenley
Hawkinge	7.5.23	56	Snipes, Grebes Siskins (1927)			12.10.27	North Weald
Kenley	17.9.32	23	Bulldogs, Harts and Demons (1933)			21.12.36	Northolt
Kenley	21.9.32	32	Siskins, Bulldogs, Gauntlets Hurricanes (1938)				
-	-	32	Hurricane	I	GZ	3.1.40	Gravesend
-	-	79	Hurricane	I	NV	12.11.39	Manston
-	-	601	Blenheim	I	UF	30.12.39	Tangmere
Manston	8.3.40	79	Hurricane	I	NV	2.7.40	Hawkinge
			Det. France 10-22.5.40				
			Det. Digby 27.5-5.6.40				
Gravesend	3.40	32	Hurricane	I	GZ	27.8.40	Acklington
			Det. Manston 10-15.5.40				
			Det. Wittering 24.5-4.6.40				
Prestwick	10.5.40	610	Spitfire	I	DW	31.8.40	Acklington
			Det. Gravesend 25.5-2.7.40				
Wittering	18.5.40	213A	Hurricane	I	AK	23.5.40	Wittering
Ch.Fenton	21.5.40	242	Hurricane	I	LE	20.6.40	Coltishll
			Det. France 5.40-20.6.40				
N. Weald	6.40	56A	Hurricane	I	US	6.40	N. Weald
Digby	27.5.40	229	Hurricane	I	RE	5.6.40	Digby
			Det. Kenley 20-27.5.40				
Wittering	9.6.40	213	Hurricane	I	AK	6.40	Exeter
Turnhouse	10.7.40	141	Defiant	I	TW	21.7.40	Grangemth.
			Det. West Malling 12-22.7.40				
Hornchurch	17.8.40	266	Spitfire	I	UO	22.8.40	Wittering
Acklingtn.	25.8.40	79	Hurricane	I	NV	8.9.40	Pembrey
Acklingtn.	31.8.40	72	Spitfire	I	RN	1.9.40	Croydon
Pembrey	8.9.40	92	Spitfire	I	QJ	9.1.41	Manston
Croydon	12.9.40	72	Spitfire	I	RN	13.10.40	Leconfield
Turnhouse	12.9.40	141B	Defiant	I	TW	25.10.40	Gatwick
			Det. Gatwick 18.9-13.10.40				
Leconfld.	13.10.40	64	Spitfire	I	SH	15.10.40	Coltishill
Coltishll.	13.10.40	74	Spitfire	II	ZP	2.41	Manston
W. Malling	6.11.40	421 Flt.	Spitfire	II	LZ	15.11.40	Hawkinge
W. Malling	7.11.40	66	Spitfire	II	LZ	24.2.41	Exeter
Gravesend	11.1.41	264	Defiant	I	PS	14.4.41	W. Malling
Manston	24.2.41	92	Spitfire	V	QJ	25.9.41	Gravesend
Warmwell	24.2.41	689	Spitfire	II	PR	26.7.41	Gravesend
Gravesend	26.7.41	72	Spitfire	V	RN	24.9.41	Gravesend
Gravesend	24.9.41	609	Spitfire	V	PR	21.11.41	Digby
Wel'gore.	20.10.41	401	Spitfire	V	YO	20.3.42	Gravesend
Castletn.	17.11.41	124	Spitfire	V	ON	3.5.42	Gravesend
Gravesend	20.3.42	72	Spitfire	V	RN		
	7.42		Spitfire	IX	RN	15.7.42	Morpeth
			Det. Martlesham 22-29.6.42				
			Det. Lympne 30.6-7.7.42				
Kirtn. I.L.	3.5.42	133	Spitfire	V	MD		
	9.42		Spitfire	IX	MD	23.9.42	Gt. Sampfd.
			Det. Lympne 30.6-7.7.42				
			Det. Gravesend and Lympne 31.7-20.8.42				
			Det. Martlesham 22-30.8.42				

PRINCIPAL UNITS

From	Date	Unit	Aircraft	Mark	Code	Date	To
P'porth.	1.7.42	19	Spitfire	V	QV	7.7.42	P'porth.
Portreath	2.7.42	234	Spitfire	V	AZ	8.7.42	Portreath
Warmwell	29.7.42	307th	Spitfire	V	MX	20.8.42	Merston
Martlesham	3.8.42	401	Spitfire	IX	YO	23.9.42	Kenley
							Det. Lympne 14-21.8.42
Drem	15.8.42	222	Spitfire	V	ZD	20.8.42	Drem
Peterhead	16.8.42	602	Spitfire	V	LO	20.8.42	Peterhead
Elginton	26.8.42	2nd	Spitfire	V		13.9.42	Goxhill
Duxford	18.9.42	609	Typhoon	1B	PR	2.11.42	Manston
Ibsley	20.9.42	66	Spitfire	V	LZ	28.9.42	Zeals
Hornchch.	23.9.42	340	Spitfire	V	GW		
	10.42		Spitfire	IX	GW	20.3.43	Turnhouse
Redhill	23.9.42	611	Spitfire	IX	FY	1.7.43	Matlaske
							Det. Zeals 26-30.9.42
Acklingtn.	8.2.43	1	Typhoon	1B	JX	11.3.43	Lympne
Turnhouse	23.3.43	341	Spitfire	IX	NL	15.10.43	P'porth
Hawkinge	21.5.43	41	Spitfire	XII	EB	28.5.43	Friston
Merston	1.7.43	485	Spitfire	IX	OU	18.10.43	Hornchch.
Staplehst.	13.10.43	401	Spitfire	IX	YO	15.4.44	Tangmere
							Det. Fairwood Common 8-18.4.44
Staplehst.	13.10.43	411	Spitfire	IX	DB	15.4.44	Tangmere
							Det. Peterhead 24.2-3.44
Staplehst.	13.10.43	412	Spitfire	V	VZ		
	11.43		Spitfire	IX	VZ	15.4.44	Tangmere
							Det. Hutton Cranswick 5-20.1.44
							Det. Fairwood Common 29.3-7.4.44
Deanland	17.10.44	91	Spitfire	IX	DL	28.10.44	Manston
Manston	10.44	229	Spitfire	IX	9R	22.10.44	Matlaske
Fairwd.C.	28.10.44	345	Spitfire	IX	2Y	1.11.44	Continent
Friston	29.10.44	131	Spitfire	VII	NX	12.44	Far East
Fairwd.C.	31.10.44	322	Spitfire	XIV	3W	30.12.44	Continent
Continent	2.11.44	340	Spitfire	IX	GW	17.12.44	Drem
Formed	16.11.44	154	Spitfire	VII			
	2.45		Mustang	IV		3.3.45	Hunsdon

OTHER UNITS

From	Date	Unit	Aircraft	Mark	Code	Date	To
-	-	H Flt.	Battle (I.A.A.C.U.)			20.9.39	Gosport
						25.1.44	Detling
			Station Flight Det. Kenley and Redhill 23.6-11.9.44				
Croydon	15.11.43	405 A.R.F.					
Canada	6.11.44	168 R.C.A.F.	C47 CB17			-	-
Disbanded at Aviand 21.8.45	10.5.46 (reformed)	600	Spitfires and Meteors (1950)			10.3.57	(disbanded)
Disbanded at Vizagapatam 10.5.46	(reformed)	615	Spitfires Meteors (1950)			10.3.57	(disbanded)
Church fenton	29.3.51	41	Meteors Hunters			31.1.58	reformed with 141S at Cottishall

Spitfire twins

THESE 18-year-old identical twins caused a great deal of confusion among fellow mechanics at Biggin Hill during the later years of the war. Fred and John Swan, seen here working on a Spitfire, were among many hundreds to be stationed at "The Bump" and they worked hard to keep the aircraft serviced and operational.

Sailor Malan certainly appreciated all the ground staff. He told them in 1943: "The pilots have always received magnificent support from ground personnel, whether their duties have been concerned with the direct servicing of aircraft at dispersals, the dirty and arduous work in the workshops, the supply of equipment for pilots, or whether they have been concerned with their payment, their clothing, their cooking or their living conditions.

"You are absolutely vital to the successful continuation and termination of this grim war".

(Photograph: Imperial War Museum)

Biggin Hill airfield in the summer of 1988 taken by Philip Lane.

Kenneth McDonough's Battle for Biggin. Hurricanes of 32 Squadron southbound over their home base RAF Biggin Hill 1940. Courtesy Pilots Pals. Prints available.

Doodlebug Alley

June 1944

ONE week after D Day, on June 13, 1944, the first four pilotless aircraft — the flying bombs, or doodle-bugs as they were often called — exploded on British soil. They crossed the coast in the early hours of the morning and one crashed at Swanscombe in Kent. During the next five weeks more than 3,000 followed, all directed against London. Suddenly, the suspense and strain was as great as in 1940, for there was little warning and no respite.

The official name for the flying bomb, or buzzbomb was the "V1"; the V stood for Vergeltung, meaning Revenge — a revenge against the Normandy Landings and a last minute attempt to direct our resources from the liberation of the Continent.

The most tragic incident occurred just a few miles from Biggin Hill. Weald House, Westerham received a direct hit and 22 children under five years old and eight female staff died. Surrounded by woods and fields, Weald House was to have been the alternative Civil Defence Control Centre for Kent in the event of an invasion. By June, 1944 it was a short stay nursery for children. Ironically, those killed came from a London school destroyed by incendiary bombs.

The V1 had been in preparation in Germany since December 1943 but many of the launching sites had been demolished by British bombers, escorted across the Channel by fighters.

The defences employed against the V1 consisted of a fighter belt at sea, a coastal gun belt, an inland fighter belt and a balloon barrage. Biggin Hill was in the balloon belt and at the end of June 1944 the station was completely evacuated. Balloon crews took over and the fields around the station were covered with winches and tents and the sky was dotted with balloons.

An enormous aerial arc of balloons covered Westerham, Tatsfield, Ide Hill and Biggin Hill and at one time there were 344 balloons flying at 4,500 feet.

Many flying bombs fell on the station, for Biggin Hill was close to "Doodlebug Alley". The married quarters were damaged, the WAAF's sickroom destroyed and on July 1, one exploded on a Nissen hut, killing three men.

By the end of August the V1 had virtually been mastered with no more than one in seven getting through. But worse was in store — the "V2", a deadly weapon that approached in silence and caused twice as many casualties. More than 500 hit the capital in the remaining seven months before the Allied Armies overran the launching sites.

In September 1944 the RAF Sections began to return and by the beginning of 1945 "The Bump" was an airfield once more.

The scene at one of the balloon sites where a flying bomb was brought down by a balloon cable. The bomb fell behind the farm building at Tatsfield, Kent. (See page 135)

OPERATIONS AND SIGNALS

SECOND
DOODLE BUGS
BALL

At the BROMLEY COUNTRY CLUB

On MONDAY, AUGUST 28th, 1944

At 20.00hrs. Dancing to 01.00hrs.   :;:   Bar till Midnight

With the Doodlebugs droning overhead, Biggin Hill organised a party. They called it a Doodlebug Ball! The ticket belongs to Doug Geer.

The first VI to be brought down by barrage balloon was at Tatsfield, Kent close to the RAF Balloon Defence site at Biggin Hill.

West of Hythe stands a huge concrete sound receiver (known as a listening post) developed at Biggin Hill to detect approaching aircraft. This one erected just before the war was never operational as it was superseded by radar.

A Few of The Few

FIFTY years on, survivors of the Battle of Britain are, naturally, fewer, but many of our heroes, reluctant though they may be to wear that title remain to inspire us. Here are some of those who served at Biggin Hill, who were generous enough to allow us to photograph them in their homes.

Air Commodore Peter Brothers CBE DSO DFC & Bar, at home in Devon with his dog Spindle. He was probably the longest serving officer at Biggin Hill, with 32 Squadron from 1936 to August 28, 1940. With his wife Annette he maintains active links with ex-colleagues and enthusiastically supports RAF charities.

Squadron Leader Harbourne Mackay Stephen DSO DFC & Bar pursued a most successful career in newspapers after leaving the RAF as Wing Commander in 1945. He returned to 602 Squadron R Aux AF from 1950-52. While serving as a Pilot Officer with 74 Squadron at Biggin Hill he was uniquely awarded the DSO.

Squadron Leader Ronald Hamlyn *DFM AFC. 610 Squadron, worked with the Save the Children Fund after his retirement from the RAF in 1957. He is pictured with his daughter Susan, granddaughter Sarah and great-grandson William. Battling against ill health he is no longer able to attend the reunions which he so much enjoyed.*

Squadron Leader Donald (Dimsy) Stones DFC & Bar, recalls with enthusiasm the camaraderie of the past. On leaving the RAF he was in the colonial service and has just had published his autobiography, "Bograt". He served at Biggin Hill with 32 and 79 squadrons.

The ruins of Weald House, Westerham which received a direct hit from a V1 in June 1944. Twenty-two children and eight staff died.

2,400 FLY BOMBS FELL IN KENT

200 MORE THAN LONDON

Official Story Of County's Ordeal

WHEN the sirens of Kent wailed in the early hours of Tuesday, June 13th, many sleepy-eyed people, clad in dressing gowns and slippers, rushed into their gardens as they heard a plane roaring overhead. It seemed in trouble.

Flames were shooting from its tail. Excitedly they shouted that another enemy bomber had fallen victim to our defences.

In the North Kent area the onlookers saw the plane plunge downward, and as it hit the ground there was a terrific explosion.

The 'plane fell on waste land in Swanscombe.

People dismissed it as an enemy bomber that had been shot down before it could release its bombs. The authorities knew better.

PRELUDE TO BATTLE

And so—two nights later—did the public, for the 'planes with the flaming tails came over too frequently to be ordinary bombers.

Quickly it was realised that the Germans were using their much-vaunted V1 weapon.

The flying bomb menace had begun in earnest—and in 80 days 2,400 of the bombs were to fall in Kent, 100 more than fell in London.

And this week, Alderman E. S. Oak-Rhind, C.B.E., chairman of Kent's Civil Defence Committee, related the story of the county's ordeal during these fiendish attacks and the typical courage with which they were faced.

MAIDSTONE SHELLED THE SAME NIGHT

This is the story he told to reporters:—

Much planning and preparation had taken place preparatory for D-Day. Local Civil Defence services had been reinforced, the County Mobile Reserve strengthened and duplicated by Regional columns, drawn from other parts of England whilst all subsidiary organisations had been reviewed and were at the highest pitch of efficiency.

D-Day came and passed. Our invasion was launched from Southampton and not from the Channel ports, and Kent seemed to be right out of the picture. Once again, as has happened so often in this war, vast and careful planning would seem to have been wasted.

The night of Monday, June 13th, passed quietly, when, at 06.48 in the early morning of Tuesday, 13th, Folkestone reporting that the town was being heavily shelled. An hour later Maidstone was also being shelled. The dual shelling seemed odd.

Towards the end of the Maidstone shelling it was reported that an airplane, flying very fast and in flames, was crossing this area heading for London.

THE FIRST OF THE MANY

At 04.20 this machine crashed at Swanscombe. The incident was reported within four minutes, and it was established as the first pilotless aircraft.

Three-quarters of a hour later a second crashed at Crouch, Meanwhile a Hun machine was spotting overhead.

As I read the riddle, the guns on the French coast shelling Folkestone in order to cloak the master gun which was shelling Maidstone, in order to divert attention from the spotting 'plane and the flying bomb.

The following night and early morning passed quietly, but shortly before midnight on the Thursday flying bombs were reported coming in in considerable numbers, 26 being shot down over Kent during the first 24 hours. The flying bomb had come and was to continue with us for some 80 days.

During the first week 101 were shot down over Kent, and it was then possible to visualise what was in store for her people.

KENT SAVED THE CAPITAL

It was obvious that London was the target and that the flying bomb was made to cover, roughly, the distance between the launching site and London. Between, all should be relatively safe.

But it was equally obvious that London could not lift a finger in her own defence, and that the fight to save London from the worst would take place, must take place, over the S.E. region of England, and Kent in particular. A hard, but inevitable decision.

Much has been said about shooting the flying bomb down over "open country."

What is this "open country"? Our coastal towns, miles of countryside dotted with villages, cottages, farms and houses. Here and there some big town.

A flying bomb exploding in the air, let alone on the ground, will strip the roof, bring down the ceilings, shatter the windows of all beneath, whether it be a cottage or 500 houses—and whether it be a cottage or a house, it was somebody's home.

So often somebody's life, taken to save London. The punishment did not begin and end with the bomb, for the county had to take a veritable hail of machine-gun bullets and cannon-shells, as well as, for a long time, the fragments of A.A. gunfire.

I have seen one of them cry as a bomb escaped and sped Londonwards, and to me this typifies Kent's attitude to London.

So throughout July the fight went on. At Swanscombe eight were killed and 32 people injured, with 30 houses demolished. At Dartford seven were killed, while Wickescombe, Ruckinge, Biddenden, Benenden, Rolvenden, Wateringbury and Otpel, to name a few, all mourned fatal casualties.

WATERY GRAVE

It would be round the middle of July that the A.A. guns were massed on the coast in a great arc, stretching from Dungeness to Dover, and here came into their own, until finally they were the greatest "killers" of all our defences.

Fully 1,000 flying bombs were shot down within and seaward of this arc, but Folkestone, Hythe and the other towns down there suffered hell.

The fight ended on Friday, September 1st, and Kent breathed a sigh of great relief—how deep each one of us only knows in his own heart.

Kent's seat? 1,388 flying bombs shot down on Kentish soil, 1,000 or more shot into the sea from her coast. 152 dead; 1,716 injured, and vast material damage.

The figure which I have given refer only to that part of Kent which is known, for war purposes, as S.E. Region, but it must be remembered that the eight areas of Erith, Crayford, Bexley, Chislehurst and Sidcup, Orpington, Bromley, Beckenham and Penge, while attached to Kent for operational and statistical purposes, are still part of the administrative county of Kent and lay within the narrowing angle which finds its apex in the centre of London.

These towns justify, if justification were needed, the point of shooting down the bomb over the more open part of Kent for from the 264 bombs which fell on them 310 people were killed and 3,302 people injured. A complete reversal of the other Kentish figures.

I think the fight of the flying bomb is over, and one can look back on it.

LONDON'S DEBT TO KENT AND SUSSEX

Was the Government right in ordering it to be shot down, shot down outside the enormous, and for wartime purposes increased London boundary? Yes. Of that there is not the faintest doubt. Every analysis to which you can put the known figures answers that question in the affirmative. London could never have won through alone, or if she had her dead would have been numbered at an appalling figure.

From the 5,000 bombs launched Kent accounted for some 2,400.

Sussex wasn't far behind that total, which means that these two counties alone took five-eighths of the danger, deliberately, on to their own heads.

London may well honour Kent and Sussex.

I began this statement by referring to the work that had been planned and prepared for D-Day and expressed the view that "it would seem to have been wasted." Wasted! Every act, every preparation, met the requirements of the flying bomb. Every service had been stretched to the utmost.

Police, National Fire Service, Civil Defence, Local Government Officers, W.V.S.—all and every service has given of its very best, but over and above all it has been the People themselves—the great and glorious People—whether a bus driver, a waitress or a housewife at home—who beat V.1. It has been indeed a People's war, and bravely have the People waged it, whether they be of London or of Kent.

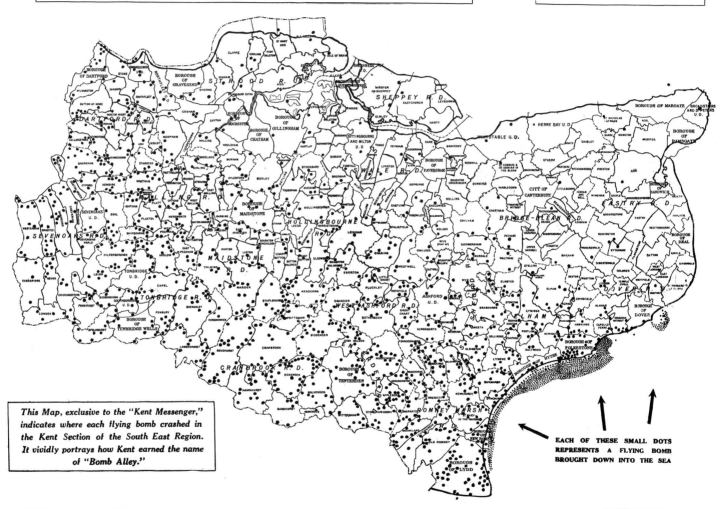

This Map, exclusive to the "Kent Messenger," indicates where each flying bomb crashed in the Kent Section of the South East Region. It vividly portrays how Kent earned the name of "Bomb Alley."

EACH OF THESE SMALL DOTS REPRESENTS A FLYING BOMB BROUGHT DOWN INTO THE SEA

Reprinted from the "Kent Messenger" (the County Paper of Kent) issue of September 15th, 1944.

Editor and Proprietor: H. R. PRATT BOORMAN, Maidstone, Kent, England.

Price 6d.

ALL PROCEEDS TO SERVICE CHARITIES.

The paper on which these maps are now being printed has become obsolete in consequence of war-time packaging difficulties and has been made available through the courtesy of Messrs. Foster Clark, Ltd., of Maidstone.

In view of the continued demand for copies, and no other paper being available, we feel sure that many people will be glad to have a map on this paper.

Where the doodlebugs crashed in Kent. Map by courtesy of the Kent Messenger.

Air Commodore Alan Deere OBE DSO DFC & Bar. DFC (US) C de G (Fr) seen here with his wife Joan. A keen supporter of the RAF Benevolent Fund, he nevertheless prefers to spend most of his time quietly at home. Born in New Zealand, he now lives happily in England.

Air Vice Marshal R. Deacon Elliott CB OBE DFC AE known as "The Deac" in 72 Squadron. He remembers the tremendous feeling of fellowship among pilots of all squadrons and the appalling loss of so many close friends. "It was certainly not 'a piece of cake'". He is proud that both his sons have passed through Cranwell. The youngest Simon has the honour of leading the British Flight of Tornadoes over Buckingham Palace on September 15, 1990. Battle of Britain Day's fiftieth anniversary.

Wing Commander Ian Cosby DFC served with both 610 and 72 Squadron at Biggin Hill. He is a great raconteur and well known to the younger generation as he still lives in Biggin Hill village. He is leading the fight to save the station and is seen here outside the Officer's Mess.

Wing Commander Jack (Bunny) Rose MBE CMG DFC was with 32 Squadron during the Battle of Britain. After leaving the RAF he had a career in the colonial service and helped bring about the status of the Cayman Islands as a tax haven. Now living in the Cotswolds he continues in community service with the Citizens Advice Bureau. Like all those involved in the Battle he values the lasting friendships highly.

Group Captain Desmond Sheen DFC & Bar., The Australian ace who settled in England after the war, seen here with his wife Rusty, takes pride in the aerobatic skills of his son, Desmond, who used to fly with the Red Arrows.

Air Commodore Dame Felicity Peake, DBE AE at home in her London flat, still leads an extraordinarily active life, both on her farm in Oxfordshire and in London as the inspiration behind the formation of "The Friends of the Imperial War Museum".

Wing Commander Douglas (Grubby) Grice MBE DFC, who served with 32 Squadron at Biggin Hill, and as Controller. He is seen here with his wife Pam who, as a WAAF at Biggin Hill was promoted to Section Officer in Codes and Cyphers. They live in Buckinghamshire and spend a great deal of time gardening.

Squadron Leader Ken Campbell DFC represents the many airmen who cannot officially be included with The Few, as they were not involved in the Battle of Britain, although they served valiantly before and after the qualifying dates. Having previously served in France, Ken was an instructor at 7 Officer Training Unit, Hawarden from June 1940 until he joined 611 Squadron at Hornchurch in July 1941 and then 72 Squadron at Biggin Hill in August.

6. RETURN OF PEACE

May 1945

FOUR years, one month and one week after the Operations Room at Biggin Hill heard an American boy, Jimmy Davies, call "Tally ho" and then shoot down a "Flying pencil" over the Channel, "The Bump" claimed its final victim of the war. Flight Lieutenant "Screwball" Buerling of 412 Squadron brought down a Focke-Wulf 190 following a raid over South Germany and took his own tally to an incredible 31.

In those four years of continuous front-line fighting, more than 1,600 enemy aircraft had been shot down by the Hurricanes and Spitfires operating from Biggin Hill. In four years the pace never slackened. When pilots were killed there were more to replace them. When Squadrons were tired, they were "rested" and another moved in.

The greatest fighter aces of the whole free world flew from "The Bump" and they were not all British. Americans, Poles, Dutch, Belgians, Czechs, Norwegians, the Free French and of course, the pilots from the Dominions all shared one common aim — to beat back, then crush, the Nazi menace.

The last few months of the war were quieter at Biggin Hill. The French and the New Zealanders were posted away to train for "Operation Overlord", the Allies' invasion of Western Europe. New squadrons moved to "The Bump" and acted as escorts to Marauders, Fortresses and Liberators. Finally, the Royal Canadian Air Force made its base there and ran a transatlantic airmail service. The country's premier fighter station was a post office!

Soon after Biggin Hill registered its "1000th kill" and then lost the charismatic Frenchman, "Rene" Mouchotte, the station's Padre, the Rev. Cecil King felt the time was right to build a permanent memorial chapel in memory of every pilot who had paid the supreme sacrifice. The chapel was housed in a disused army hut and dedicated on Sunday September 19, 1943 by Station Commander, Sailor Malan. During the service he unveiled a Reredos, made of oak which bore the names of Dunkirk, Dieppe and the Battle of Britain and contained the names of every pilot who took off under the colours of the Biggin Hill Wing, never to return. The pulpit was made by a local carpenter and a policeman from Sevenoaks carved the astral crown and wings. A Book of Remembrance was beautifully lettered and illuminated by the CO of the RAF Regiment Airfield Defence Unit.

There was one final victory for Biggin Hill. A victory for Great Britain and a victory for freedom. On May 7, 1945 the Germans surrendered and, in time-honoured tradition, a great party was organised on "The Bump".

This was their finest hour.

ROYAL AIR FORCE STATION

BIGGIN HILL

SERGEANT'S MESS
VE DINNER

Now it is over, and we can modestly claim that we have played at least a small part in the successful termination of the European war, and in the establishment of something which found its beginnings in the earliest days of the struggle, burst into vigorous life in the Battle of Britain, bloomed luxuriously during the sweeps of 1941, '42 and '43, and clung tenaciously to existence during the battle of the flying bombs — the Biggin Hill tradition.

FRIDAY, 15th JUNE, 1945

In the Biggin Hill tradition a dinner was organised in the Sergeant's Mess to celebrate the Allies' victory in Europe. Inside this menu, Biggin Hill proudly declares — 'We played our part well'.

Memorial to The Few

July 25, 1951

This photograph of the ruined chapel of St George's was taken on December 3, 1946 after fire had totally ravaged the building. The cause was never discovered. (Photograph: RAF Biggin Hill)

AFTER all the losses during the Battle of Britain, the bombing of the station and the offensives over Western Europe, Biggin Hill continued to be haunted by ill fortune, even in peacetime. In 1946 the little memorial chapel, which was in daily use as the station church, caught fire and was totally gutted. The cause was never discovered and little was salvaged from the ruins, except the charred visitors book in which one name was still legible — Winston S. Churchill.

Padre Cecil King immediately devoted his energies to the building of a new Chapel — a purpose-built building in memory of the pilots who died. He became the driving force behind an appeal and contributions came from all over the world.

At first it was planned to redesign and convert the old operations room, blitzed and evacuated in 1940, into a new St. George's Chapel of Remembrance. The plan was changed and the site of an old hangar on the North Camp, near the main road, was chosen. The Chapel was built in a rich red brick with a large barn-style roof in heavy terra cotta tiles, the tower with a small roof to match. Inside a very special tranquillity was created, the severity and simplicity personified in the plain brick walls.

The Chapel contains 12 stained glass windows, each telling a story, depicting the spirit of Biggin Hill. There are the badges of the seven squadrons who served at The Bump during the Battle of Britain, the badges of Fighter Command, No 11 Group and the Station and there are portraits of the immortal Spitfire and Hurricane. Each window was donated.

Four hundred and fifty three aircrew were killed while flying from the Biggin Hill Sector between 1939 and 1945 and they came from 52 Squadrons. Their names are inscribed on the oaken reredos to each side of the altar. The gilded wooden eagle on the lectern, the altar crosses, the alms dish and the candlesticks were all gifts from the friends of Biggin Hill.

The Foundation Stone was laid by Air Chief Marshal The Lord Dowding on July 25, 1951 and the Service of Dedication conducted by the Lord Bishop of Rochester on November 10, 1951. For almost 40 years, St George's Chapel, unique in RAF history, has been the regular place of worship for the airmen and their families who live and work at Biggin Hill. Many thousands of visitors from all over the world have walked through its doors to experience for themselves the deeply moving reminder of the spirit and selfless dedication that took Britain through its most crucial years in history.

In the whole of the Free World there is no better memorial to The Few.

The windows in the Chapel of Remembrance were designed by Hugh Easton. Here we have parachute packing, aircraft servicing, rescue services and ground control. The Chapel contains 12 windows and each was donated.

The St George's Chapel of Remembrance with the guardian Spitfire and Hurricane, taken before the building of the main block for the OASC which was erected on the site of the large Belfast hangar and parade ground.

Permanent Memorial

SEPTEMBER 20, 1954. When Dr Chavasse, Bishop of Rochester dedicated two veterans of the war, a Hurricane and Spitfire, as a permanent memorial to The Few, the service held on the concrete apron in front of the hangar was attended by more than 5,000 people.

The Bishop in his sermon said: "In these very skies overhead the flower of English youth put paid to the German hopes of invasion, though often to the cost of their glorious young lives. There was, in war, an urgency. There was an exhaltation and an adventure that brought out all that was noblest in the national character".

There was another tribute on that late summer day in 1954. Twelve Meteors dipped in salute over the station, sweeping only 100 feet high over St. George's Chapel of Remembrance. The picture shows the entrance approach to the Chapel in 1955 with the guardian Spitfire and Hurricane. The Foundation Stone is set in the wall beneath the west window.

No more flying

1946-1958

ON the last day of July, 1946 the Auxiliary Air Force was reformed and two Squadrons, 600 (City of London) and 615 (County of Surrey) flew in to enjoy post-war peace at Biggin Hill. With them came a mix of Spitfires, FR14s, F14s and F21s. The "Weekend Air Force" soon reached peak efficiency and in 1949 reverted to Fighter Command, although not as front-line units.

In 1950 the Auxiliaries were re-equipped with Meteor F4s followed by F8s the following year. In March 1951 they were joined by 41 Squadron with Meteor 8s, and Biggin Hill became a fighter station for the last few years of its RAF flying life. The sleek Hawker Hunter, direct descendant of the immortal Hawker Hurricane, was introduced and the station brought up to full operational strength.

The decision in March 1957 to reconstitute the Auxiliary Air Force meant the end of 600 and 615 Squadrons. For a year, 41 flew on alone, but in a world of rapid advances in aviation technology, of rockets and guided missiles, its days were numbered. There was no need to locate manned fighters in the crowded air space.

On January 16, 1958, 41 Squadron was disbanded. It reformed the same day at Coltishall equipped with Javelins, and amalgamated with 141 Squadron.

141? Wasn't that the number of the "Cock Squadron" which won the Concours d'Elegance for Biggin Hill way back in 1918? Wasn't it the Squadron which flew Defiants in the Battle of Britain and was virtually wiped out? Wasn't it the Squadron which made a great come-back with Night Fighters.

As far as history is concerned it was a tidy way to say goodbye to flying at RAF Biggin Hill. But nobody at the time considered that little irony. They were too busy listening to the silence which had settled across the valley below "The Bump".

The Hawker Hunters and Meteor 8s of 41, 600 and 615 Squadrons at Biggin Hill in 1956. One year later the Auxiliary Squadrons were disbanded in the interests of economy, a decision which came as a bitter blow to the 'Weekend Air Force'. (Photographs: Joe Merchant)

Sydney Camm's sleek Hawker Hunter of 41 Squadron, a direct descendant of the immortal Hurricane, comes in to land. The end of flying at RAF Biggin Hill is near.

The spirit lives on   *1959-1990*

FROM a front-line fighter base Biggin Hill became headquarters for the Ground Officer Selection Centre whose staff moved from Uxbridge to occupy the North Camp accommodation in April 1959. They were joined three years later by the Aircrew Selection Centre, thus concentrating the whole selection process under one roof.

Biggin Hill was still operational — but only for one day each year. On a weekend close to September 15, when in 1940 Hitler sent over massive formations of bombers and fighters in his bid to "wipe the RAF from the map", the station opened its gates to the public and staged a spectacular "At Home" display. In the early days the spare-time pilots from 600 and 615 Squadrons put the Meteor through its paces and then, in stark contrast, such old-timers as the Bristol Fighter and the Sopwith Pup. But the biggest cheer of all was always reserved for the aircraft which helped Britain win the war.

In 1976 the Ministry of Defence made the financial decision to scrap the Biggin Hill display and in September more than 100,000 people came to "The Bump" to see the Spitfire and the Hurricane, flying by courtesy of the Battle of Britain Memorial Flight.

In 1961 the South Camp was leased to Surrey Aviation and became the home of numerous private flying clubs. Under the management of Squadron Leader J.R. Maitland who was one of the first pilots to break the sound barrier, Biggin Hill became a thriving civilian airport. At one time there were more than 250 light aircraft based there and movements totalled more than a ¼ million a year.

The ownership of the airfield passed from the Air Ministry to the Civil Aviation Authority and finally to Bromley Borough Council which paid £450,000 for the site in June 1973 and encouraged small business aircraft and executive jets.

It was, however, the small flying clubs which adopted the wartime spirit of "The Bump" and on four occasions in the 1960s they took part in a "Longest Day" competition which was based on a typical 1940 scramble and continued from dawn to dusk.

Mr David Porter's Flairavia Club was victorious on three occasions out of four and he is still a proud custodian of the "Longest Day" cup. There were major differences. For all their competitiveness on the ground and expertise in the air these enthusiastic flyers of the sixties did not receive one chilling message over the R/T which told them there were "bandits at 10 o'clock". Nor did they bale out into the Channel, hoping a rescue launch was nearby. Nor were they taken prisoner in France and locked away in Stalag Luft 111.

But the spirit of Biggin lived on; in fact it never left.

Group Captain Dick Grice returns to the White Hart to see the famous blackout screen, with him is landlady Kath Preston.

Just a victory roll away....

THE White Hart at Brasted, the second Mess during the war for most of the squadrons, was not far from The Bump. Through the village, down Westerham Hill, along the A25 and there it was. A homely inn, full of character. By air it was just a victory roll away.

Kath Preston, who was 'mine host' throughout the war, still remembers the faces of those whose laughter filled the bar and those who were not ashamed to cry when a friend failed to return. Mrs Preston, recalled how Group Captain Dickie Grice "found" her pub when he was Commanding Officer.

"I need somewhere for the boys to relax. Somewhere where they can let their hair down", he said.

The boys would swoop down the road in convoy with Dickie leading the way in a small bus complete with loudspeaker. "Calling the White Hart." he would bellow from 200 yards away. "Set up 25 beers and 26 eggs and bacon". (There was always one non drinker).

There was usually something to celebrate — like the time Johnny Checketts walked into the bar, 45 hours after he had been reported missing. Like the Sunday lunchtime when Stanford Tuck left his beer on the counter and said: "Keep it warm. I'll be back". He rushed to Biggin Hill, flew on a sortie, shot down two planes, and was back before closing time. Like the night Al Deere told the boys he was getting engaged. Like the night "Bush" Bandidt won an old car at darts....and it blew up when he started it.

There were bad nights too. The nights of the missing faces when Mrs Preston quickly learned not to ask questions. She recalled the day early in the war when Lance Bowler, a peace-time pilot confided to her — "I'll never come through this little lot". He didn't. He was one of the first casualties.

It was Dickie Grice who had the idea of signing his name on the blackout screen. "Don't let anybody but my men sign it", he asked. Nobody did, except for two soldiers billetted in the village. Their names were scrubbed out.

As the war progressed, more and more "aces" came to the White Hart to add their illustrious names to this unofficial memorial. After the war the board was framed and unveiled by Sailor Malan.

As they drank their beer and talked, raids, bombs and aircraft were forgotten. So too was closing time and the village policeman frequently had to be called to persuade them that even under extraordinary circumstances, the drinking hours had to be respected. "Time to leave", he would tell them. "You can always come back tomorrow".

For some, of course, there was no tomorrow.

The "Red Knight" returns. Wing Commander Michael Crossley finds an old haunt – and the landlady's still there.

Air Fair spectacular

BIGGIN Hill's historic contribution to aviation progress is reflected today in the spectacular Air Fair which attracts crowds in excess of 100,000. In fact it is one of the most popular two-day summer events in the country.

When, and if, the RAF leaves Biggin Hill people will still flock to this famous old fighter station each June to see the top-quality pilots and the exciting aircraft that keeps the U.K. among the leaders in world aviation.

One day the Concorde and the Harrier will only be seen in museums, alongside the Bristol Fighters, the Gauntlets, the Hurricanes and Spitfires. Future generations will see the miracles of the next century flying, we hope, from Biggin on The Bump.

Adolf Galland, the Luftwaffe General who ended the war as Germany's top fighter ace, was a surprise visitor to the White Hart where he spoke about the chivalry which existed between the two sides. Galland was the man who wined and dined Stanford Tuck on the day he was shot down and then struck up an unusual but lasting friendship. Galland is pictured here with some of those he met in combat. In the foreground from left to right: Galland, Tony Bartley, Brian Kingcome, Neville Duke and Bob Stanford Tuck.

On Thursday July 16, 1959, Sailor Malan, then 48 years old, returned to Biggin Hill for the first time since the war. Quite naturally he popped into The White Hart with Tubby Mayne (right) and Jamie Rankin (left) meet landlord Teddy Preston. This was to be Sailor's last trip to England. Returning to his ranch in South Africa, he lived another few years before dying of Parkinson's Disease. Alan Deere was his last wartime colleague to see him alive. He flew to his farm at Kimberley and met Malan, his wife Linda and son Jonathan. "I stayed with the family for about two hours. It was a sad occasion. . . .I have never been so moved and the memory of that day still remains with me" — Alan Deere said. Sailor Malan died in 1963.

The full group, as they were at the White Hart reunion . . .
1, Mrs. Kathy Preston; 2, Group Captain Kent; 3, Mrs. Betty Rose;
4, Group Captain Ryder; 5, Air Vice Marshal Robert Deacon Elliott;
6, Wing Commander Jack "Bunny" Rose; 7, Mrs. Helen Kingaby;
8, Wing Commander Kingaby; 9, Group Captain Kingcome;
10, Miss Patricia Kingaby; 11, Wing Commander "Tich" Havercroft;
12, Wing Commander Stanford Tuck; 13, Squadron Leader "Gandy"
Drobinski; 14, Flight Lieutenant Martel; 15, Wing Commander
Paddy Barthropp; 16, Air Commodore Wootten; 17, Air Commodore
Duke-Woolley.

The men who used to pile out of the bus, sink their pints and tell Kath Preston how their day had gone, returned to the White Hart on Sunday September 14, 1969 — the day before the premiere showing of the film, Battle of Britain. They are pictured here, 29 years older, less noisy and looking anything but what they were — fighter pilots with 138 officially recorded "kills" between them.

In October 1949 The Queen visited 600 Auxiliary Squadron. Biggin Hill has enjoyed many royal occasions but this was a big day for "The Bump" and 600 Squadron was delighted to welcome its Honorary Air Commodore. (Photograph: Quadrant Picture Library)

I walk with ghosts

1990-1992

DURING one of his last visits to Biggin Hill, Winston Churchill spoke once more about the spirit and the will of the people who had refused to lie down and be beaten when Britain was in a desperate crisis. "This station", he said "must never close".

Some years after Churchill's death the Government confirmed an earlier decision to close the camp, sell the site and move the RAF Selection Centre to Cranwell, retaining only the Chapel of St. George's as a symbol of the historic role played by the station in the Battle of Britain.

A few days after the Secretary of State for the Armed Forces had made his announcement, another Battle of Biggin began, with all the determination of old. There were suggestions that it should become a museum and a petition, signed by over 14,000 people, including many former fighter pilots, was delivered by Wing Commander Ian Cosby to 10 Downing Street. It was all to no avail. RAF Biggin Hill is due to close in 1992 and Churchill's words may go unheeded.

The fact remains that Biggin Hill is the most famous of all the centres of the Battle of Britain and the memory of its role is etched deeply in our history. This stretch of flattened fields and conglomeration of huts, barracks, administration buildings, hangars and workshops is something rather special. It is the heart of our very existence as a nation.

More than 200 decorations for gallantry were won by the pilots flying from "The Bump". They include the DSO, DSC, DSM and the George Medal. They include the MBE and the Military Medal for four WAAFS. They include American and European awards too numerous to list. They include the Freedom of the City of London and, of course, the Borough of Bromley. But more important than any award is the memory of the 453 aircrew who lost their lives flying from the Biggin wing. They represent the Commonwealth and twelve allied nations.

Brian Kingcome in his foreword to this book says: "I lost many old friends. . . .and the worst part was watching them die, spiralling down with a smudge of smoke, or breaking up, watching for a parachute to blossom, the relief when it did, the sick feeling when it didn't. I walk with ghosts when I re-visit my old station. . .".

For the sake of the next generation . . . and the next . . . and the next . . . "Biggin on The Bump" should never close.

RAF Biggin Hill. Sir William Stanier's Class LM5MT 4-6-0 Locomotive No. 45110 being named at Bridgnorth on 12th September 1971, with a guard of honour from RAF Cosford. This was the last steam locomotive to pull a passenger train for B.R. and was saved from the scrapyard by Mr David Porter an ex-RAF Biggin Hill man together with Air Commodore. Peter Brothers and Group Captain T.P. Gleave who presented it to the Severn Valley Railway where, after overhauling and re-furbishment, the naming ceremony took place. Not to be confused with Battle of Britain class locomotive No.34057 BIGGIN HILL which had previously been scrapped despite Mr. Porter's attempts to save it.

Commanding Officers

Major Orme
OC Wireless Testing Park Joyce Green —
Moving to Biggin Hill in December 1916
1916 — August 1917
Major H.B.T. Childs
OC Wireless Testing Park
Later Wireless Experimental Establishment
August 1917 — May 1918
Colonel L.F. Blandy, DSO
OC Wireless Experimental Establishment
April 1918 — December 1918
W/Cdr G.P. Grenfell, DSO
OC Wireless Experimental Establishment
December 1918 — November 1921
Major P. Babington, MC
OC 141 Squadron
January 1918 — June 1918
Major B.E. Baker, DSO
OC 141 Squadron
June 1918 — June 1920
S/Ldr I.T. Lloyd
OC 56 Squadron
November 1922 — September 1923
S/Ldr Sir C.J.Q. Brand, KBE, DSO, MC, DFC
OC 56 Squadron
September 1923 — August 1925
S/Ldr F.J. Vincent, DFC
OC 56 Squadron
August 1925 — September 1926
S/Ldr Elliott-Smith, AFC
OC 56 Squadron
September 1926 — January 1928
The Station was closed for rebuilding
between 1928 — 1932
W/Cdr G.B. Dacre, DSO
October 1932 — January 1933
W/Cdr E.O. Grenfell, MC, DFC, AFC
January 1933 — February 1937
W/Cdr H.G.W. Lock
January 1937 — November 1938
W/Cdr R. Grice, DFC
November 1938 — December 1940
G/Cpt F.O. Soden, DFC
December 1940 — June 1941
G/Cpt P.R. Barwell, DFC
June 1941 — July 1942
G/Cpt J.R. Hallings-Pott
July 1942 — December 1942
G/Cpt A.G. Malan, DSO, DFC
January 1943 — October 1943
G/Cpt H.L. Maxwell, CBE, DSO
November 1943 — February 1945
W/Cdr L. Raphael, DSO, DFC
February 1945 — April 1945
G/Cpt M.W.S. Robinson CBE
April 1945 — June 1945
W/Cdr E.D. Crundall, DFC
June 1945 — September 1945
W/Cdr C.M.H. Outram
October 1945 — May 1946

W/Cdr G.J. Spence
May 1946 — June 1947
S/Ldr G.J. Gray, DFC
June 1947 — December 1947
S/Ldr G.D. Sise, DSO, DFC
December 1947 — May 1948
W/Cdr D.C. Smythe, DSO, GM
June 1973 — February 1976
W/Cdr A.H. Donaldson, DSO, DFC, AFC
September 1950 — January 1952
W/Cdr W. Pitt-Brown, DFC, AFC
January 1952 — February 1953
Wing Comander D.G. Smallwood,
   DSO, MBE, DFC
February 1953 — October 1955
G/Cpt J. Barraclough, DFC, AFC
October 1955 — February 1957
W/Cdr P.D. Thompson, DFC
February 1957 — January 1958
S/Ldr R.S. Salmon
January 1958 — March 1958
W/Cdr H.W.G. Andrews, DFC
March 1958 — January 1959
S/Ldr R.S. Salmon
January 1959 — February 1959
S/Ldr E.F. Lapham
February 1959 — April 1959
G/Cpt G.P. Seymour- Price, DFC
May 1959 — June 1959
G/Cpt G.N. Amison
July 1959 — February 1962
G/Cpt R.B. Morison, DFC, AFC
February 1962 — April 1962
S/Ldr G.N. Bray
April 1962 — November 1962
W/Cdr R.C. Everson, OBE, AFC
November 1962 — November 1964
W/Cdr L.F. Wolsey
November 1964 — July 1967
W/Cdr I.L. McCombie
October 1967 — March 1970
W/Cdr P.E. Prior, OBE, AFC
March 1970 — June 1970
W/Cdr M. Scholes, MBE, DFM
June 1970 — June 1973
W/Cdr R. Gebbels
June 1973 — February 1976
W/Cdr K.J.O. Balsillie
February 1976 — September 1977
W/Cdr A.L. Wright
September 1977 — April 1979
W/Cdr J.R. Myers
April 1979 — June 1981
W/Cdr F.J. Smith June 1981 — August 1984
W/Cdr D.C. Boak
   August 1984 — November 1986
W/Cdr C.I.B. Skellern B.Ed
November 1986 — October 1988
W/Cdr A.D.G. Jones AFC
   December 1988 —

Throughout the preceding pages of this book, the glorious spirit of RAF Biggin Hill shines out, not only as an example to all of us who still serve in the Royal Air Force, but to everyone who cherishes the freedom won for us by the gallant 'Few'. In today's uncertain and changing world, that freedom can only be assured by constant vigilance and by the professionalism of our future airmen and airwomen. Although the aircraft have left Biggin Hill the station continues to play a vital role in maintaining the defence of our freedom. All those who aspire to be tomorrow's officers and aircrew attend a rigorous selection procedure at the Officers and Aircrew Selection Centre and only the very best are accepted into the service to follow in the footsteps of those who have gone before them. The future of the Royal Air Force, and indeed our freedom, will be in their hands as we move towards another century. From what I have seen of them, they will not fail us and they will be worthy successors to the Few.

AIR COMMODORE
G R PITCHFORK MBE BA

Air Officer Commanding and
Commandant Officers and
Aircrew Selection Centre,
Royal Air Force, Biggin Hill.

Royal Air Force Biggin Hill is soon to close with its' present main function, the Officers and Aircrew Selection Centre being moved to Royal Air Force Cranwell. However, we all look back with great pride and affection to the glorious achievements of the Biggin Hill Squadrons and groundcrews of the past, who, through their exceptional courage and fortitude, helped to turn the tide in the 'Battle of Britain'. The station is very different now, the famous 'airfield on the bump' has been run as a civil airport for a number of years and South Camp is now the nucleus of civil flying activities, but the old North Camp remains and Royal Air Force Biggin Hill still occupies some of the buildings that formed part of the wartime station. This book brings back the atmosphere and emotions of the war years and is a fitting remembrance in the 50th Anniversary Year of the Battle of Britain.

WING COMMANDER
A D G JONES AFC

Present Station Commander
Royal Air Force Biggin Hill

Three heroines walk past the bomb battered buildings. A photograph taken in 1940 of (left to right) Sergeant Elizabeth Mortimer, Corporal Elspeth Henderson and Sergeant Helen Turner, all recipients of the Military Medal. Miss Turner died in 1947 but Mrs Elspeth Green (formerly Henderson) and Miss Mortimer returned to the Station in 1974 to attend a ceremony in which three roads in the married quarters were named in their honour. (Photograph: Imperial War Museum)

Three of today's WRAFs are photographed as they walk past the building which replaced the badly bombed offices of 1940. Adopting the pose of their predecessors are: (left to right): Corporal Jenny Mitchell, Flight Lieutenant Verena MacLean and Sergeant Fiona Evans. They may be among the last WRAFs at "The Bump".

THEY PAID THE SUPREME SACRIFICE

STATION COMMANDERS
G/Cpt Philip Reginald Barwell DFC
G/Cpt Gordon Raphael DSO DFC

No 350 (BELGIUM) SQN
P/O Frederick Leopold Boute
Sgt Albert Michel De Hepcee
F/Sgt Gaston Louis Ghislain Dancot
F/O Jean Jules Victor Gerard
F/O Albert Michel Leon Herreman
F/Lt Robert Andre Guy Alexandre
F/lt Francois Venesoen DFC

No 32 SQUADRON
F/O Lancelot Gordon Bowler
P/O Geoffrey Inglesby Cherrington
P/O Keith Reginald Gillman
P/O Kenneth Kirkcaldie
S/Lt Geoffrey Gordon Bulmer FAA

No 80 SQUADRON
F/O Robert Hawksley Hanney
P/O William Edmund Maloney
F/O Peter Struan Haw
W/O Peter Leopold Godfrey

No 85 SQUADRON
P/O Stanley Philip Benge
F/Lt Arthur Bickerstaffe Woods AFC
2/Lt Jan Otto Richard Bugge
P/O George Grevile Gilling LAX DFC
Sgt Harold Norman Howes DFM
Sgt Robert Scott Hutton
F/O Donald William Owen
F/Lt John Peter Marley Lintott DFC
Lt Per Adolph Thoren
S/Lt (A) Jack Arthur Thomas Parker
W/Cdr Henry Woodhouse DFC AFC
F/Lt Walter Weir
S/Lt (A) Thomas Holland Blundell

No 129 (MYSORE) SQN
F/Lt Philip Norman Howard

No 315 (POLISH) SQN
W/O Tadeusz Jankowski
S/Ldr Eugeniusz Horbaczewski DSO
F/Lt Henryk Stefankjewicz
W/O Jan Adamiak
F/O Stanislaw Calinski
F/Lt Adam Sworniowski
W/O Kazimierz Siwek

No 277 SQUADRON
Sgt William George Bunn
F/Sgt John Stanley George Arundel
F/Lt George Grant-Govan

No 92 (EAST INDIA) SQN
Sgt Eric Thomas George Frith
P/O William Charles Watling
Sgt Stanley Herbert Vinter
Sgt Gordon Charles Waldern
Sgt Charles Gordon Todd
Sgt Kenneth George Port
F/Sgt Charles Sydney
Sgt Frederick Edgar Postlethwaite
P/O Ernest William Harry Phillips
F/Lt James Alfred Paterson MBE
Sgt Kenneth Bruce Parker
Sgt Trevor Guest Oldfield
F/O Abergonway John Pattinson
Sgt Gerald Edgar Francis Scawen
Sgt Ernest Harvey Roff
P/O Desmond Gordon Williams
F/Lt John Wilfred Lund
P/O Patrick Alexander Learmond
Sgt Paul Henry Klipsch
Sgt Henry Stanley Harrison
P/O Howard Perry Hill
Sgt Grahame Edwin Hann
P/O Frederick Norman Hargreaves
Sgt Trevor Roger Gaskell
Sgt Peter Raoul Eyles
Sgt Henry Norman Edge
P/O Harry Davies Edwards
F/O John Fraser Drummond DFC
Sgt Herbert Cox
P/O Basil Bartholomew
P/O John Bryson
Sgt Leslie Charles Allton
Sgt John Ahenn

No 486 (R.N.Z.A.F.) SQN
F/Sgt David Buchanan Clark
P/O Jesse Pearse
P/O James William Waddell
P/O Alexander Alfred Wilson
P/O Roland John Wright
F/O Leslie Vincent Weir

No 441 (R.C.A.F.) SQN
P/O Victorien Gilbert Brochu
F/O Alexander McDonald

No 66 SQUADRON
Sgt Charles Albert Henry Ayling
P/O George Henry Corbett
F/Lt Kenneth McLeod Gillies
F/Sgt Maurice William Hayman
Sgt Peter Hamilton Willcocks
F/O Peter Christopher King
P/O David Alexander Maxwell
P/O John Romney Mather
P/O Peter Raymond Mildren
P/O Hugh William Reilley
P/O John Alnod Peter Studd
P/O Laurence George Stone
Sgt Arthur Dumbell Smith
Sgt Frank Ernest Waller
Sgt Rufus Arthur Ward

No 33 SQUADRON
Lt Anthony Geoffrey Askew
F/Lt Ernest Edward Tribble

No 406 (R.C.A.F.) SQN
F/O Ralph William Donovan
F/O Charles Hamlyn-Lovis
F/O Victor Martin Grant
P/O Kenneth Bradley Hicks
F/Lt John Ballantyne Kennedy
F/O William Frederick Kilpatrick
F/O Elmer Adrian Oswald
F/Lt Robert John Radcliffe
F/O Reginald Arthur Henry Allen
F/Lt Thomas William Trewin

No 154 SQUADRON
F/O Albert Harding Hurst

No 141 SQUADRON
Sgt John Frances Wise
F/O Denis Conon Williams
Sgt Albert George Curley
Sgt Robert Crombie
Sgt Frederick Peter John Atkins
F/Lt Ian David Grahame Donald
P/O Arthur Charles Hamilton
P/O Rudal Kidson
P/O John Richard Kemp
P/O Richard Alexander Howley
F/O Geoffrey Colman Pledger
P/O Dudley Malins Slatter

No 65 (EAST INDIA) SQN
P/O Noel Rees Macqueen
Sgt Robert Raistrick Law

No 41 SQUADRON
Sgt Walter Raymond East
Sgt John Islwyn Thomas
F/Lt Thomas Rex Poynton
F/Sgt Clifford Oddy
F/O David John Shea
F/Sgt Roger Lee Short
W/O Peter Warren Chattin
F/Lt Rijklof Van Goens

No 29 SQUADRON
Sgt Ralph Edmond Wilson
P/O Alan Grout
F/Sgt Roger Hall
Sgt Francis Paul Miller
P/O John Murray Pope
F/O Charles Robert Miles
Sgt David Graham Patterson
F/O George Pepper DFC & Bar
Sgt William Gordon Pengelly
P/O Anthony Nelson Prior
P/O Alexander MacGregor Mitchell
Sgt Browne Ryall
P/O Joseph Henry Toone DFC DFM
P/O Reginald Neville Walford
Sgt Eustace Harry Whitmee
F/Lt Cyril Walter Oxborrow
F/Lt Joseph Eric Bennett DFC
F/O Henry William Ellis
F/Lt Ronald Richard Densham

No 485 (R.N.Z.A.F.) SQN
F/O John Albert Ainge
P/O Fraser Dudley Clark
F/O Murray Metcalfe
W/O Herbert Samuel Wipiti DFM
Capt John Robert Walker

No 2 SQUADRON
F/O Bernard Cyril Tasker
F/Lt William Anderson Black AFC

No 133 (EAGLE) SQN
P/O William Albert Arends
P/O Ben Perry De Haven
P/O Dick D Gudmundsen
P/O William Kenneth Ford
P/O David Ray Florance
P/O Grant Eugene Eichar
P/O Fletcher Hancock
P/O Carter Woodruff Harp
F/Lt Coburn Clark King
P/O Moran Scott Morris
P/O Gilbert Inland Omens
P/O Robert Lewis Pewitt
P/O Seymour Morton Schatzberg

No 316 (POLISH) SQN
Sgt Marian Szmit

No 609 (WEST RIDING) SQN
Sgt Guy Alexander Chestnut
Sgt Kenneth Walter Bramble
F/Sgt Geoffrey Charles Bennett
F/O Joseph Dawson
Sgt Alan Ronald Newnham Davis
F/Lt John Curchin DFC
P/O Douglas Lindsay Cropper
P/O Sydney Jenkyn Hill
F/O Raymond Dopere
P/O Rudolphe De Grunne
Sgt Philippe Maurice Macsherry
Sgt Robert Turner Mercer
F/Lt Dudley Persse-Joynt
Sgt Arthur Gordon Palmer DFM
Sgt Ernest Walter Pollard
F/Sgt Stanley Herbert Spallin
P/O Thomas Douglas Leslie

No 349 (BELGIAN) SQN
F/Sgt Albert Etienne Van Den Broeck

No 611 (WEST LANCASHIRE) SQN
S/Ldr Hugo Armstrong DFC
F/O David Fulford DFC
Sgt John Richard Gilbert
F/O Paul Ernest Helmore
Sgt George William Keans Kraus
F/O Gordon Rowland Lindsay
Sgt Robert Maxwell McLay
F/O Victor Stephenson Neill
P/O Jonathan North
F/S Allan Edgar Pearce
Lt Rolf Torbjorn Tradin
Sgt Alton Ronald Mackay
W/Cdr James Hogarth Slater

No 26 SQUADRON
F/O William Arthur Phillips
F/O Henry Peter Steel

No 74 (TRINIDAD) SQN
Sgt Thomas Brian Kirk
F/O Peter Cape St John
P/O Robert Smith
F/O Alan Leslie Ricalton
P/O Denis Norman Evelyn Smith
Sgt John Alan Scott
S/Ldr Eric John Michelmore
Sgt Neil Morrison
P/O John Howard
P/O William Garbutt Henderson
P/O Douglas Hastings
P/O Michael Frederick Halahan
P/O Harold Raymond Gunn
Sgt John Nixon Glendinning
Sgt Laurence Eric Freese
F/Sgt Leslie Raymond Carter
P/O Peter Chesters
P/O Donald Gordon Cobden
P/O Edward Walter Churches
S/Ldr John Mungo-Park DFC & Bar
P/O William Walker Burgon
P/O Richard Dennis Aubert
Sgt David Hart Ayers
Sgt John Rex Bergis White

No 3 SQUADRON
F/O George Edward Kosh
F/Sgt Stanislaw Domanski
F/Sgt Donald John Mackerras
S/Ldr Kenneth Wigglesworth DFC

No 1 SQUADRON
P/O George Carson Whitmore
Sgt Harris Robert Fraser
F/O Cyril Leslie Bolster
P/O James Duncan Fairbairn
P/O Sidney Daniel Cunningham
F/O Joseph Maurice Chalifour
F/Sgt Leslie Ernest Watson
F/Sgt Godfrey Tate
W/O Edward Reuben Andrews
F/O Thomas Wyllie

No 616 (SOUTH YORKSHIRE) SQN
W/O Donald Arthur Gregg

No 610 (County of Chester) SQN
P/O Kenneth Henry Cox
S/Ldr Alexander Franks AFC
Sgt Peter Douglas Jenkins
F/O Graham Lambert Chambers
F/O Gerald Malcolm Theodore Kerr
F/O John Kerr Wilson
P/O Frank Kinnersly Webster
F/Lt William Henry Warner
F/Sgt John Henry Tanner
S/Ldr Andrew Thomas Smith
P/O Arthur Lionel Boultbee Raven
Sgt William John Neville
F/O Albert Rupert John Medcalf
Sgt William Thomas Medway
Sgt Edward Manton
P/O Peter Litchfield
F/Sgt Ingvar Frederick Hakansson
F/O George Mercer McKinlay

No 504 (Country of Nottingham) SQN
W/O Reginald Charles Bolland

No 401 (R.C.A.F.) SQN
P/O Gerald Bickle Whitney
F/Lt James Whitham DFC
F/O Clarence Alfred Blake Wallace
F/Lt John Richards Tucker
F/Sgt Stanley Lewis Thompson
P/O Sydney Frank Smither
P/O John Allan Small
F/Sgt William Ellis Rowthorn
P/O John Randolph Patton
P/O Lyman Edward Hokan
F/Sgt William Dewey Hagyard
Sgt Robert Walter Gardner
P/O Jack Kenneth Ferguson
F/Sgt Frank Alexander Duff
Sgt Gerland Francis Clarke
Sgt Morton Haist Buckley
Sgt Alexander Douglas Blakey

No 306 (POLISH) SQN
F/Sgt Tadeusz Josef Koloszczyk
P/O Feliks Migos
P/O Egon Stanislaw Zygmund

No 501 (County of Gloucester) SQN
P/O Pawel Zenker
P/O Edmund John Sylvester DFC
F/Lt George Edward Bowes Stoney
F/O Arthur Thomas Rose-Price
Sgt Geoffrey Wilberforce Pearson
F/O Kazimierz Lukaszewicz
Sgt Oliver Vincent Houghton
P/O A.E. Van Den Hove D'Ertsenryck
P/O Duncan Alexander Hewitt
P/O Frederick Cecil Harrold
P/O Edward Maurice Gunter
P/O Vilem Goth
Sgt Edward James Egan
Sgt Frederick John Dixon
F/O Philip Anthony Neville Cox
P/O John Wellburn Bland
F/O Nathaniel John Barry
P/O Hugh Charles Adams
P/O Frank John Vid
F/Lt Cyril Thornton MBE

No 340 (FRENCH) SQN
P/O Marcel Renaud
F/Lt Eugene Reilhac
S/Lt Jacques Moreac
F/Sgt Paul Hubidos
F/O Emile Claude Helies
S/Lt Charles D'Autichamp

No 605 (County of Warwick) SQN
F/Lt Arnold John Craven DFC
F/Lt Richard Maitland Singer
F/Sgt Leonard William Woodard DFM

No 322 (DUTCH) SQN
W/O Justin Albert Maier
F/O Baron Van Nagell
F/Sgt Cornelius Kooy
F/O Rudolph Frans Burgwal
F/Lt Jan Leendert Plesman
F/O Gilles Pieter De Neve
F/O Lambertus Douwes Wolters

No 451 (R.A.A.F.) SQN
F/Lt John Desmond (Barney) Wallis

No 229 SQUADRON
F/Lt Patrick Edgar Brownie
P/O Georges Louis Doutrepont
F/O Malcolm Ravenhill
F/O Geoffrey Mervyn Simpson
F/Lt George Mains
Lt Robert Alexander Cumming
W/O Harold Gore Head
F/Lt Walter Doornink Idema

No 56 (PUNJAB) SQN
P/O Ross Carrock Richard Lean
F/O Thomas Guy Atkinson
F/Sgt Anthony Clayton Drew

No 79 (Madras Presidency) SQN
P/O James Joseph Tarlinton
P/O Stanislaw Piatkowski
F/O George Charles Boyce Peters
F/O Edward William Mitchell
Sgt Ronald Revan McQueen
S/Ldr John Davies Clement Joslin
F/Lt Richard Willoughby Reynolds
P/O John Edward Randell Wood
P/O Lionel Roger Dorrien-Smith
F/Lt James William Ellias Davies DFC
Sgt Henry Cartwright DFM
Sgt Henry Albert Bolton
P/O Llewellyn Lister Appleton

No 410 (R.C.A.F.) SQN
F/Lt Ralph Henry Jackson
P/O Murdoch Campbell Murray

No 91 (NIGERIA) SQN
P/O Noel Proctor Warden
P/O Edwyn Tonge
Sgt Frederick Aaron Thornber
Sgt Edwin Edward Sykes
F/Lt William Boyd Opr
Sgt Willie Mitchell
F/O James Gilbert Johnson
P/O Douglas Hugh Gage
F/O Ronald Gordon Vicary Gibbs
F/O John Baxter Edwards
P/O Melville Kerson Eldrid
W/O Richmond Anthony Blumer
P/O Raymond Kenneth Wildish
F/Lt John Denys Fletcher
F/Sgt Andrew Smitton Darling
P/O Jacques Coudray
Sgt Jack Charles Chittick
P/O Irvin William Downer
F/Lt Arthur Gerald Donahue DFC
F/O Henri Jean Marc de Molenes
F/O Raymond Gustave Dehasse
F/O Gordon Harry Dean
Sgt Gerald William Baker
P/O Archibald William Black
F/Lt Alan Andrews DFC & Bar
F/Lt Jean Pierre Maridor DFC
F/O Kenneth Roy Collier
F/Lt Eugene Georges Seghers DFC
F/O Patrick Alfred Schade DFM
S/Ldr Norman Arthur Kynaston DFC
S/Ldr George St Clair Boyd Reid
F/O John Arundel Collis

No 341 (FRENCH) SQN
Sgt/Ch Yves Bourges
F/Sgt Pierre Magrot
Comdt Rene Gaston Mouchotte DFC
Lieut Philippe Beraud

No 96 SQUADRON
Lt/Cdr (A) Patrick Humphreys GC RN
F/Sgt Hamilton Maurice Lynes
F/Sgt William Allen Pavey
F/Sgt William Milne Patterson
F/O John Cecil Owen Allan
F/O Robert Douglas Warren
F/Sgt David Motherwell

No 274 SQUADRON
F/Lt George Joseph Aylott
F/O Norman James Purce
F/Sgt Royston William Ryman

No 124 (BARODA) SQN
P/O Francis Henry John Ashton
F/Lt Svatopluk Bachurek
P/O Marie Joseph Robert Larcher
Sgt Zdenek Kothera
F/Lt Jaroslav Kulhanek
F/Sgt Thomas Campbell MacFarlane
P/O Edward Noel Macdonell
P/O Basil Craig Middleton
Sgt Cyril George Pritchard
P/O Michael Gordon Meston Reid

No 165 (CEYLON) SQN
F/Sgt Harold Thomas Wise
W/O Albert Edquard Zevaco

No 213 (CEYLON) SQN
Sgt Antoni Wojcicki
Sgt Geoffrey Norman Wilkes
F/Lt Ronald Derek White DFC
Sgt Sidney George Stuckey
F/Lt Lionel Harold Schwind
P/O Jacques Arthur Philippart
Sgt Philip Purchall Norris
P/O Joseph Emile Laricheliere
P/O Richard Ralph Hutley
Sgt Samuel Leslie Butterfield DFM
P/O Maurice Simon Henri Buchin
P/O Harold Derrick Atkinson DFC
F/O William Napier Gray

No 242 (CANADIAN) SQN
P/O John Benzie
P/O Norman Neil Campbell
P/O Kirpatrick Sclanders
F/O Michael Giles Homer DFC

No 72 (BASUTOLAND) SQN
P/O Douglas Cyril Winter
F/Sgt David Richard White
S/Ldr Herbert Richard Tidd
Sgt Charles Leonard Thompson
P/O Norman Sutton
F/Lt Dudley Stewart-Clark
Sgt Leonard Stock
F/Sgt William David Sherriff
Sgt Robert Patrick Reilly
F/O Oswald St John Pigg
F/O Brady Oscar Parker
Sgt John Graham Merrett
F/Sgt John Grant McCutchan
P/O Ernest Edward Males
Sgt Raymond Frederick Lewis
Sgt Charles Leslie Harrison
P/O Dennis Frederick Holland
Sgt Philip Thomas Grisdale
F/O Jerzy Godlewski
Sgt Malcolm Gray
P/O Leonard Basil Fordham
P/O Robert Plumpton Frahm
Sgt Edwin George Enright
Sgt Dennis William Davies
F/O Paul John Davies-Cooke
Sgt Allan James Casey
F/O Edgar John Wilcox
P/O Herbert Robert Case
P/O Noel Edwin Bishop
Sgt Albert Frederick Binns
F/Sgt Tom Watson
P/O David Owen Waters

A Book of Remembrance in St. George's Chapel contains the names of all the aircrew of the Biggin Hill sector who gave their lives, and the date on which they died. Every day a page of the book is turned by the duty airman — a deeply moving reminder of the selfless dedication which helped to take Britain through those crucial years. The names of the 453 aircrew of 52 Squadrons who paid the supreme sacrifice are also inscribed on a Reredos in the Chapel. Sir Winston Churchill in a commendation of this shrine said:

‘ **My personal association with Biggin Hill during the Battle of Britain lives in my mind. As a nation we have short memories and it is as well that memorials such as this should bring to our remembrance the cost of our victory in the days when one of our fighter pilots had to be worth ten. They died without seeing the reward of their efforts; we live to hold their reward inviolate and unfading.** ’

The second world war was Winston Churchill's finest hour. His personal strength and determination in the face of a seemingly impossible task inspired all the airmen at Biggin Hill, just as it inspired the whole Free World. On September 5, 1954 the Prime Minister inspected 615 (County of Surrey) Squadron. He then presented them with the Esher Trophy for the most efficient Auxiliary Squadron in the RAF. (see right) Just another small victory for Biggin on The Bump.
(Photograph: Quadrant Picture Library)

The author

Bob Ogley is the author of the book *In the Wake of The Hurricane* which covered the trail of the storm to hit southern England in October 1987. It became a national bestseller, remained in the top ten for eight consecutive months and was highly acclaimed by critics all over the world.

In 1989 Bob retired as editor of the Sevenoaks Chronicle, a weekly newspaper in Kent to concentrate on his own publishing business which he established after his first book was rejected.

Through the sales of his books Bob has raised in excess of £50,000 for a variety of woodland appeals. His royalties as author of Biggin on the Bump will go the the RAF Benevolent Fund.

Bibliography

RAF Biggin Hill **Operations Record Book, Squadron Diaries, RAF Biggin Hill** by Graham Wallace, **The Bump** by Nicholas Wright, **Battle of Britain Then and Now,** edited by Winston Ramsey, **Men of The Battle of Britain** by Kenneth G. Wynn, **Kent Airfields in the Battle of Britain**, by the Kent Aviation Historical Research Society. **Grandfather's Biggin Hill** by John Nelson, **Thanks for The Memory** by Laddie Lucas, **The Battle of Britain** by Richard Hough and Denis Richards, **The Mouchotte Diaries, The History of Air Fighting** by Air Vice Marshal Johnny Johnson, **The Bromley Times** Personal Papers and Letters. Ministry of Defence Air Historical Branch.

Biggin on the Bump

What the pilots say . . .

"Brings back more memories than any other book . . . pure nostalgia in print and pictures." — **Wing Commander Jack (Bunny) Rose, MBE CMG DFC**

"a most real and descriptive account of events at that time. Interesting, exciting but with a vein of sadness throughout, especially for one who was there." — **Air Vice Marshal R. Deacon Elliott, CB OBE DFC AE**

"I congratulate you on its high standard and content. It is a first class record and brings back many memories" — **Air Commodore Peter Brothers, CBE DSO DFC & Bar**

"splendid . . . a really marvellous book" — **Wing Commander Brian Kingcome, DSO DFC**

"It is indeed a superb publication and one which I am sure will command tremendous interest. I think Brian Kingcome's article most moving and exceptional in its content." — **Group Captain Desmond Sheen, DFC & Bar**

Other books from Froglets

In The Wake of The Hurricane (Kent Edition) . . . . . ISBN 0-9513019-0-X £7.00
In the Wake of The Hurricane (National) . . . . ISBN 0-9513019-18 . . . . . £7.50
In the Wake of The Hurricane (Hardback) . . . . ISBN 0-9513019-4-2 . . . £11.95
Surrey in The Hurricane . . . . ISBN 0-9513019-2-6 . . . . £7.50
Hurricane Gilbert . . . . ISBN 0-9513019-5-0 . . . . £7.50
London's Hurricane (Paperback) . . . . ISBN 0-9513019-3-4 . . . . £7.95
London's Hurricane (Hardback) . . . . ISBN 0-9513019-8-5 . . . £11.95
Eye On The Hurricane – Eastern Counties
(Paperback) . . . . ISBN 0-9513019-6-9 . . . . £7.95
Eye On The Hurricane – Eastern Counties
(Hardback) . . . . ISBN 0-9513019-7-7 . . . . £11.95
King Oak of Sevenoaks – A childrens' story . . . . ISBN 1-8723379-00-7 . . . £6.95

In the Wake of the Hurricane

What an inspired idea to cover the hurricane's trail. This really is a magnificent book. — **Group Capt Sir Leonard Cheshire VC**

"We chroniclers of the storm all stand in debt to Bob Ogley in much the same degree as all other epic poets stand in debt to Homer" — **George Hill, Hurricane Force.**

"It is indeed a remarkable record of a dreadful night and a record which will become part of the history of our country" — **Denis and Margaret Thatcher, 10 Downing Street.**

A first class production and an excellent record of the devastation that hit our part of Kent on the night of October 16, 1987. Bob Ogley has put it together with great speed and commendable skill. — **Winston S Churchill, Westerham.**

Literary fate has made him a star — something he declines being at his roots a country-man who has pumped his typewriter and cracked his staff into action over the past 18 years. Because of demand In The Wake of The Hurricane is more elusive than Spycatcher. — **Exeter Express and Echo.**

As a record of the power of nature mocking the efforts of man and as a reminder of the vulnerability of things we take so much for granted this is an awesome volume. — **Kev Reynolds, Environment Now**